The Police Writing Handbook

A guide to effective report writing for UK policing
professionals

Ann Ellis

ELLIS-HALL
Publishing

Published by **Ellis-Hall Publications**, 58 Rivington Ave, St Helens, WA10 6UE, England

Cover design: Jimmy Davies
http://jimmydaviesportfilio.com/

Printed by Poplar Service Print Ltd,
Poplar House, Jackson St, St Helens, WA9 3AP

Dedication

This book is dedicated to my late parents,
Frances and Ellis Hall.

They would have been proud.

Table of Contents

Chapter 2: **The Basics**

Chapter 3: **The mechanics of language – Punctuation**

Chapter 4: **Spelling**

Chapter 5: **The dos and don'ts of good report writing**

Foreword

As a former Superintendent in South Yorkshire, and a police officer for thirty two years, I have experienced at first hand how the burden of paperwork associated with each case has increased year on year. I have also seen how costly badly written reports and case files can be in terms of budget, with time wasted in checking and rewriting. In addition there is the possible failure of cases in court because of incomplete or unclear written evidence.

This book is an excellent tool not only for police officers and detectives, but also for police specials, PCSOs and the wide range of civilian staff who also prepare reports and case files which must be read by a wide audience.

I found the book easy to follow with clear explanations and exercises. Common errors are illustrated through examples from police writing. Some of these made me laugh, as I recognised them from my own writing as well as that of others with whom I have worked.

Writing in the Police Service is full of jargon and acronyms. We follow old established ways, simply because that's the way we were taught, with bad habits being passed down as each generation of new recruits joins the service. As a result, our writing is often stuck firmly in the past.

It's now time to move into a new era of professional, clear police writing and I believe this book will help enormously in achieving that aim.

Ret Superintendent Christine Wallace
South Yorkshire Police

Preface

Most people would agree that writing skills are vital within the workplace in general. However the role of the police officer and that of other investigative officers is particularly 'language rich' and has unique needs and requirements. From initial notes and statement writing through to file preparation and case summaries, police officers are required to use written language skills in a variety of circumstances and for multiple audiences. All of these language events are highly specific to the sector, so where do police officers turn if they want to improve the quality and efficiency of their workplace writing?

For the past twenty years I have been delivering workplace training in English language skills to police officers and other investigating professionals. Many of my students have told me that the emphasis on the written word and the need for accuracy within the justice sector has reawakened their insecurities about grammar, punctuation and spelling. They have stated that they felt embarrassed about asking for help and have struggled along, with paperwork adding to the stress of their everyday job roles.

During classes, students asked about a wide variety of concerns, from where to place an apostrophe, to whether to use 'affect or 'effect'. I jotted all these queries down for addition in subsequent classes, and it is these notes that have been the springboard for this book. However, I did not want to write just another grammar book, so I carried out research into exactly what police officers, and other police staff, needed to write and the problems they faced. I talked to retired officers, joined policing forums and even accosted police officers walking the beat in my own area to ask for their opinions and suggestions for the book. They have all played a part in the production of this book and I hope that as a result it will help to make the working day easier and less stressful for dedicated men and women in the modern Police Service.

Acknowledgements

I would like to thank Ret. Detective Superintendent Christine Wallace, who has offered support and answered my questions throughout the writing of this book. I would also like to thank the serving officers who have read the manuscript and offered valuable comments and suggestions. As serving officers, they cannot be named, but you know who you are. In addition, I would like to thank Anne Smith, Glenn Allan and the numerous other people who have proofread and checked my work (any remaining errors are all mine) and Jimmy Davies for the cover design. Last but not least I would like to thank my husband Bob, without whose loving support and encouragement, this book would never have been written.

Introduction

So step forward those of you who joined the police service to write reports and fill in forms. No one? Ok, one… there's always one. The truth is that people join the Police Service for a whole list of reasons but ploughing through mountains of paperwork is rarely one of them.

Do you find yourself struggling to complete file preparation and reports, given tight deadlines and a busy schedule? Do your reports get returned for the correction of spelling or grammar errors or for structural revision? Do you lack confidence in your written reports or feel dissatisfied with the quality of your writing? Do you think you would benefit from some guidance to make writing tasks easier, quicker and more professional?

By working through this book you will refresh your knowledge of English grammar and dispel some of the myths surrounding 'rules' that you learnt at school. You will discover how understanding the way English language works will give you greater control over your writing, making it simpler but more effective. You will learn strategies to improve your spelling focussing on words that are relevant to your role as police officers and staff. Police writing is unique and you will develop skills to write sector specific reports that are clear, complete, effective and professional.

I wrote this book because the police officers who attended my English language training sessions said that they would like a book that would help them to refresh their existing knowledge, develop new skills and provide ongoing reference materials to help with their daily writing tasks. Throughout the writing process, I have consulted with serving and retired police officers, whose suggestions and advice have contributed to a book that is not only an effective writing handbook, but one which is relevant to the writing requirements of modern policing.

As you work through the book, you will see that each section has clear explanations of the topic being studied. There are exercises with answers to help you to check your own knowledge and skills as you progress through the chapters. There are also learning tips that will help you to remember important points. Although the book has been designed as a progression route, you might just want to dip in to the areas that you feel least confident with; the book's structure allows you to do this too. In addition, it has been written with your job role in mind so whether you want to use it as a course book, a refresher of certain topics or as a reference book for times when a question arises, you will find that it meets your individual needs.

You will see that the correct grammatical terms are used throughout. This is because many people say that they learn better when they can attach labels to writing structures. In addition, these terms now form part of the new literacy curriculum in primary schools so those of you who help children with schoolwork can get a head start. For those of you who hate learning terminology, don't worry; there are more familiar terms and examples to help you to work your way through the book in a way that suits you best.

A police officer's writing might be read by a number of people including supervisors, legal professionals and jurors. If you want to feel confident that your writing is accurate, clear, effective and complete for all audiences, turn to the first chapter: 'The Why, Who and What of Police Writing'

Chapter 1

The Why, Who and What of Police Writing

Objectives:

At the end of the chapter you will:

- be able to write for different audiences, purposes and formats
- be able to write a narrative in first and third person
- demonstrate an understanding of objective versus subjective language
- be able to write an effective summary
- be able to write an effective email

Introduction

We have already seen that a considerable amount of a police officer's time is spent in writing. Notes, statements, reports, general administrative tasks, which all contribute to an ever-increasing mountain of highly specialised writing tasks. The problem is that although most people learn to read and write at school, when they begin to work within the criminal justice system, they find that different skills are needed to write effectively in this environment.

Before considering what and how you write as a modern police officer, we can identify a number of basic requirements necessary in your reports. An effective police report must be accurate, concise, objective, clear and complete. In later chapters we will see how to achieve this through correct grammar and punctuation as well as a clear writing style. In this chapter, we will look at police writing tasks in general; what you need to write, whom you are writing for and why. The aim is to focus on the general themes in your writing before moving on to the mechanics involved in the process.

Purpose, audience and format

Those of you who have completed an English language course such as GCSE or Functional Skills might remember the acronym **PAF**:

Purpose
Audience
Format

This acronym gives a good place to start when considering the breadth of writing needed in your workplace. Most of us write more in our everyday lives than our counterparts of twenty years ago. This is because the range of communication devices at our disposal that transmit textual content, has increased at such a rate that it has, in some ways, exceeded our capacity to adapt and develop workable writing practices. Many police officers have described finding time in a busy day to complete writing tasks, only to log on to their emails and find dozens of messages, some of which might even be from someone sitting at a nearby desk or in the next room; some will be urgent and some not, but all have to be read to make that distinction. This eats into the little time available for writing statements and reports. This 'information overload' can be detrimental to both health and performance. It is therefore vital to think about how we write in order to consider how these tasks can be carried out more efficiently.

Before we consider specific workplace writing tasks, think about the texts that you produce during the course of a single day (personal as well as work related) and make a list of them. There will probably be a wide variety of types of text that you produce, including emails, text messages, post it notes, formal reports and so on. You could use a table like the one below for your list. I have added a few examples from my typical day to illustrate:

Purpose	Audience	Format	Features
To **inform** someone of a meeting	A colleague	email	Facts, clear language
To **persuade** someone to meet for lunch	A friend	text	Informal language, exclamation marks, short/incomplete sentences, XXs
To **advise** someone how to correct an essay	A student	Internet forum	Formal but friendly, lists, examples
To **inform** someone how to address spelling problems	Police officers	Book chapter	Formal, subheadings, bullet points, tables

You can use the table below to add some examples of your own:

Purpose	Audience	Format	Features

If you look at your completed list, you should notice that the purpose (why you are writing), the audience (who you are writing for) and the format (what you are writing) will all influence your writing style, language and layout (features). In many everyday writing tasks, understanding these relationships help to make writing more successful. In the next section we will look more closely at these planning tecniques and see how making the right decisions can make writing more efficient and more effective.

Does your writing have a clear purpose?

Most text is produced with a general purpose in mind, such as to inform, to persuade or to advise. In addition, each text will have at least one specific purpose that identifies what you want to achieve with the text. You might write an email to a colleague to persuade them to join a darts team; a message to a supervisor to inform them of where you will be; or a letter to a community group advising them about feeling safe in their homes. Once you have defined the purpose of your writing, you can start to think about the audience.

Using audience analysis to make your writing effective

In police writing many of the documents produced have several audiences, for example, other police officers, other legal professionals or members of the public. It is vital for effective writing that you understand your audience. You can carry out a basic audience analysis by asking yourself the following questions:

- Who will be the audience for a text?
- What do they already know about the subject?
- How much do they need to know?
- How do you want them to react/respond?

Thinking about your reader in this way helps you to focus your writing, making it more concise and improving clarity. This advice is simple to follow when you are writing to an individual or a group of people who share knowledge of the issues being discussed or the language used within your workplace. However, much of police writing is more complicated than this, with multiple audiences for a single text. If you consider your own statement on an MG11, how many audiences might read it? The table below illustrates its journey (*continued on the next pages*):

Format	Audience	Profile
Statement MG11	Supervising officer	Police officer – • will have knowledge of the case • have knowledge of similar documents • understand police jargon • understand police language
	Police legal team – preparation of case files	Police officer/civilian • have knowledge of similar cases • have knowledge of similar documents • have some knowledge of police jargon • have some knowledge of police language

	CPS – decision on whether to prosecute	Legal professional • have knowledge of similar cases • have knowledge of similar documents • have some knowledge of police jargon • have some knowledge of police language
	Legal teams – solicitor/barrister – defence and prosecution	Legal professional • have knowledge of similar cases • have knowledge of similar documents • have some knowledge of police jargon • have some knowledge of police language • have expertise in manipulating language to support or challenge an account • knowledge of the above might be limited

	The jury – decision on guilt or innocence	Lay person • limited knowledge of similar cases • little knowledge, if any, of similar documents • limited knowledge of police jargon - usually from TV • limited knowledge of police language – usually from TV

We can see from the table above that even in this narrow selection of people through whose hands your document might pass (you could probably identify more), there are wide differences in the understanding of how you write and what you write. In cases of multiple audiences like this, it is advisable to identify the primary decision maker/s.

In the journey of your statement or case summary, there seem to be two points where important decisions are being made. The first lies with the CPS, who must decide whether there is enough evidence to proceed with a prosecution. However, these are legal professionals who work closely with the police and have a solid understanding of what the documents is for and as well as familiarity with police language. The second is with the jury. A jury is made up of twelve people (fifteen in Scotland) who are chosen at random from the electoral role. The majority of jury members will have little experience of the justice system or the language involved in the processes.

As these people are major decision makers, it is essential that you think of them as your primary audience. You might not be called to give evidence in a trial, so your statement, which may be read out, must be clear, coherent and unambiguous to the jury because you will not be there to clarify verbally.

Constructing a narrative

In the last sections we considered the purpose and the audiences involved in police writing. In this section, we will examine the format; in other words the form that the writing takes.

In UK policing, almost every act that an officer carries out has to be documented in some way. There are an alarming number of forms, over twenty in the MG suite alone, that officers and staff must complete as part of each case. In some cases these forms have a pre set format with spaces to enter specific details. As part of your initial, classroom, or on the job training, you will have been given guidance about what the forms are for and what needs to be written in them. This book does not aim to cover those practical aspects of your day-to-day writing, however, there are many writing tasks that require officers to write a narrative of what has happened, for example MG5, MG11, emails, memos, press releases etc. Officers on my courses tell me that even with guidance during training, they find this type of writing time consuming, difficult to construct and the result is often disorganised. This section aims at developing a template to plan and carry out narrative writing to help you achieve clear, organised and coherent text that you will feel confident about.

As human beings, we are predisposed to construct narratives as a way of ordering things and making sense of the world. We recount stories all the time: our day at work, our near miss in the supermarket car park, or an altercation with a neighbour. Usually, these narratives are littered liberally with exaggerations, opinions, and suppositions, and in some cases - lies, all of which would be totally acceptable in an everyday story but have no place in police narratives. However, narratives, whether stories such as those above, fictional narratives or those found in police reports share the same structural features and this can be the start of your narrative writing framework.

Every police report must address three concerns: the investigation, the action taken as a result, and the case status. In a police narrative, the aim is to record information as succinctly, yet as informatively as possible. Therefore the report should address the following questions:

1. **WHO** - Who did what to whom? who is involved in this case? Name the victims, suspects, and witnesses.
2. **WHAT** - What happened? What crime was committed? What was taken? What was used to commit the crime?

3. WHEN - time of day, day of week, month, and year.
4. WHERE- Where was the crime committed? Where was the weapon found? Where was the victim taken?
5. HOW - How was the crime committed?
6. WHY - What is the motive of the crime?

(Of course, initial reports might not be able to answer the last two questions).

Exercise 1.1

read the following police narrative to find answers to the above questions:

On 10-08-14, at approximately 1915 hrs, I was dispatched to 14
Sycamore Avenue, New Town, following a call from a concerned neighbour (Marie Pritchard) about a domestic dispute.

Upon arrival I determined that an argument had took place between John Davis (husband), Jennifer Davis (wife), and George Davis (stepson/son). During the argument in their house, John pulled a knife on George in a threatening manner. George then pulled a baseball bat and struck John.

Paramedics took John to hospital. George was later arrested and charged with assault with a deadly weapon.

Who was involved? _____

What happened? _____

When did it occur? _____

Where did it take place?_____

Why was the officer called? _____

How did the injury occur? _____

Although the above report answers the questions, it still has gaps. What's missing? After reading the report, what do you not know? Imagine that you are either the CPS or a defense/prosecution barrister. What additional information would you need to prepare for the case?

Adding detail

A case can come to trial years after your report was completed and the chances of remembering what you meant by vague sentences such as 'some valuable objects were stolen' is very remote. Therefore, it is vital that the narrative contains sufficient detail in order to be effective as evidence.

Exercise 1.2

Read the report below and underline any vague statements.

Several incidents of theft had been reported in relation to the warehousing unit. The most recent occurrence that I attended resulted in an injury to an individual who needed medical treatment. This individual reported being knocked over by a person dressed in dark clothing. A witness said that she had heard a noise and found the rear doors open and items missing.

For further practice, try re-writing the following vague sentences

1. The suspect stole expensive items from the shop.

   _____

2. I checked the scene for evidence

   _____

3. The fire in the house caused substantial damage

   _____

4. I proceeded in a northerly direction after the suspect.

   _____

After writing your narrative, you can use the following checklist to help you make sure that it is complete and correct:

After you have written the narrative, use the checklist below to be sure it is complete and correct.

✓ Narrative clearly states the crime/event that occurred.

✓ Narrative identifies the scene (time and place).

✓ Narrative summarizes the crime/event in chronological order (beginning, middle, end).

✓ Narrative includes details about what was SEEN.

✓ Narrative is factual (objective).

✓ Narrative contains correct spelling.

✓ Narrative contains correct capitalisation.

✓ Narrative contains correct punctuation and grammar.

In addition to being clearly written, police reports should be easy to follow. In order to achieve this, officers rely on transitional words to convey sequence, cause and effect, emphasis, addition and results. In my work with police officers, I have noticed that some people use the same words over again. In a long narrative, this can become boring and meaningless. The table below gives some alternatives that you could use to keep your writing interesting.

Purpose	Transitional Word
Sequencing ideas	Initially, first, second, next, last, following, later, after, then, while
Cause and effect	because, since, thus, therefore, due to this, as a result of, consequently, in order to
Example	for instance, for example, another
Adding a point	next, in addition, besides, not only . . . but also, similarly
Contrasting	but, instead, yet, however, on the other hand, in contrast, whereas, still
Summarising	to summarise, therefore, in summary, to sum up, consequently, therefore

First person or third person?

In some of your writing tasks you will be expected to write in the first person, and in others in the third person. Because formal grammar has not always been taught at school, some officers say that they are not sure what these terms mean and how they differ. Here is a quick guide to help you.

When we talk about 'person' we are really talking about point of view. A first person account would be written from your own point of view and would include pronouns such as *I, me, we, us my, mine, our* and *ours* (we will cover parts of speech in more detail in chapter 2). In other words, you are narrating an event that you were part of, from your own point of view. This is the form that you should always use when writing an MG11 or any narrative that documents your personal involvement in an incident.

A third person is the point of view of someone outside the action. Even if you were personally involved, as is often the case in police writing, you must imagine yourself as an observer. You will use pronouns such as: *he, she, it, they him, her, it, them his, her, hers, its, their* and *theirs*. You would use this form when writing an MG5 because the MG5 is a summary of the case as a whole, not just your own involvement.

Many officers say that they find it difficult to write in the third person for MG5s. They have been advised by colleagues to copy and paste text from MG11s and MG3s and where appropriate, just change 'I' to 'he/she' throughout. This is not an effective way of compiling this document and there are a number of problems that result from this practice. Firstly from a grammatical perspective, simply changing the pronouns obscures the meaning in a sentence. Look at the extract adapted from an MG11 below:

I also explored the fact that the venue regulates the two floor capacities and I asked him how they regulate it currently. He answered by saying that they are never at full capacity anyway.

If we cut and paste this in an MG5, it is very difficult to follow:

*He also explored the fact that the venue regulates the two floor capacities and **he** asked **him** how they regulate it currently. **He** answered by saying that they are never at full capacity anyway.*

(adapted from brighton-hove.gov.uk)

Even in this short extract, it is not clear to see who is asking the questions and who is replying; imagine this repeated throughout the narrative.

Another problem associated with this practice is that cutting and pasting from several documents results in a lack of coherence. We have seen in this chapter, the importance of a clear and logical account and this can't be achieved in this patchwork fashion.

In addition to a lack of clarity, cutting and pasting from other documents does not provide a true summary. Solicitors often complain that there is not enough information, with key points missing. Alternatively, there is too much information to be able to pick out they key points in the time they have before going into court. Worse still, it might contain information that they would have preferred not to disclose at that time. Remember, the MG5 narrative might start before your involvement in it, cutting and pasting could result in the loss of that information.

The advice therefore is to write an MG5 from scratch, following the structures outlined in this chapter. Imagine that you are an impartial onlooker in this case. Extract the key points and organise them into a coherent order using one of the planning techniques already outlined and write your third person account as if you were another officer, using he/she, they etc. Although you might think that this process is more time consuming than simply cutting and pasting, it will save time ultimately, as you are less likely to have to re write it. In addition, you can feel confident that when the case goes to court, the summary will be concise, clear and objective.

Subjective or objective

Subjective language is that which deals with thoughts, opinions, bias and judgements. On the other hand, **objective** writing is observable, based on facts supported by evidence. Police writing is usually required to be objective and many writers find it quite difficult to write objectively as the line between subjective and objective writing is sometimes very narrow. We can easily identify the following example as subjective:

He said that my question had confused him. I can't imagine what was so difficult about it.

The writer here is clearly making a judgement about the man's ability to understand his question and it is easy to turn an objective statement into a subjective one by adding a few words without really thinking about it. For example:

She refused to tell me who had attacked her. (objective)

She didn't want to tell me who had attacked her. (subjective – the writer has made a judgement about the victim's feelings)

To avoid subjective language, use your senses; say what you saw, heard, smelt etc:

Subjective	Objective
Scruffy	torn shirt, dirty jeans, brown stains
afraid	hands shook, eyes wide
drunk	failed a breath test
reckless	drove at 70mph on a road with a 30mph speed limit, mounted the pavement

Be aware of objective and subjective language:

Subjective

S/he does not want to
S/he does not like
S/he thought
S/he feels
S/he thinks
S/he needs
S/he was trying to get me to
S/he was trying to get out of

Objective

I saw
I counted
I observed

S/he said
S/he did this…
The noise s/he made sounded like…
S/he made an action that looked like…

A word on summarising.

It seems obvious to say that a summary is a shortened version of a longer text or group of texts. Many police personnel have told me that they find it very difficult to summarise and often end up with a text that is longer than the original. This is a common problem wherever writing takes place. The following general tips on summarising will help you to carry out the task more successfully:

- Read the original text thoroughly to make sure that you understand its over all meaning.
- Use a dictionary to help you find the meaning of any unfamiliar words.
- Underline or highlight the main points of the text, ignoring any unnecessary facts, descriptions or opinions. Make a note of the most important details - you could even draw a diagram, flow chart or use pictures if it helps at this planning stage.
- Organise your key points under sub headings to aid coherence. These can be removed later if your department does not allow this format.
- Summarise by linking together the key points using sentences or paragraphs as appropriate.
- A summary does not need to contain information, descriptions or opinions that do not support the general meaning of the text.

- Read your draft to make sure that you haven't lost the over all point of the original information. Make amendments to your draft as necessary.

Learning tip

- A written summary should be a brief, 'easy to read' version of a longer piece of writing.
- It must contain the main points of the original text and it should be written in your own words. Don't just copy out 'chunks' of the original version.
- You should write your summary using correct grammar, punctuation and sentences.

Writing emails to get results

In most workplaces, much of our communication is achieved through emails and this is certainly the case in policing, with messages sent to colleagues, outside organizations and members of the public.

We now use emails in a very different way from what was intended when the first one was sent in the 1970s. The fact is that for much of the time we don't even think of these communications as emails, instead we treat them as part of a conversation. This is because, with the availability of mobile communication devices such as smart phones, tablets and smart watches, we are checking our messages on a regular basis; in queues, in the lift and even in the bathroom. This view of emails results in a lack of structure, as we tend to 'think' on screen rather than consider how to construct our message. Whilst we think we have sent a message that is clear and has all the relevant information, the recipient is confused, frustrated and sometimes angry because they are unable make complete sense of our communication. This can lead to communications becoming increasingly unhelpful or worse still, ignored altogether. This situation can be improved by concentrating on structure because this forces you to organise your thoughts effectively.

The key to structure is SCRAP. This stands for:

Situation
Complication
Resolution
Action
Politeness

The following email outlines how SCRAP works in practice:

Dear Rebecca

Thank you for a very productive briefing this morning. We covered a lot of ground in a short time.

Situation – You should open your email with something that your reader can agree with. This establishes empathy and puts your reader in a positive frame of mind.

The bad news is, I have just been informed that the police budget for this community initiative has been cut by 25%. This means that we will have to rethink some of the projects we have been discussing.

Complication *– This is the issue that needs addressing. If you start with this, you risk alienating your reader.*

Don't panic too much yet because the Community Action Group have come up with some funding ideas that should cover most of the cuts.

Resolution *– here is something that can be done to solve the problem. This might just be a suggestion.*

I will draft an action plan and timetable so that we can stay focussed on where we are up to.

Action *– positive steps to be taken by the reader, the writer or another individual.*

Thanks again for your help – let me know if you need more information.

Politeness *– ends the email on a positive note. Makes the reader feel appreciated.*

Kind regards

PC George Dilworth
Community Liaison Officer

You can see that although this email contained bad news, it was delivered in a constructive manner. This is much more likely to get a positive result from the reader. In real world writing, messages are likely to be much more complicated than this example but it will still be possible to identify the SCRAP elements. If your message has more than one problem, you should offer a resolution to the first one before outlining the next one and so on.

Conclusion

This chapter has encouraged you to think about what you write, who you write for and the format and structure that you use to construct your writing. Police writing must be clear, efficient, thorough, professional and objective. Remember that you and your profession will be judged by your writing.

The chapter has also offered frameworks around which to structure your writing. Although this seems like a lot to think about when time is tight, the guidance here will actually save you time in having to rewrite. In addition, the more you think about your writing as part of a structure, the quicker the whole process will become.

The way police officers use language, especially in writing, is different from the average layperson; you may be unaware of this because you are immersed in the culture and language associated with policing. The following chapters will help you to make your writing comprehensible and professional so that everyone in the chain has a clear understanding of what you want to say.

The next chapters look at the basics of writing, grammar and punctuation. Much of the ambiguity in writing is caused by a lack of understanding of how the language works at these basic levels. Chapter four gives some guidance on spelling rules and tips for remembering how to spell certain types of words. Chapter five aims at developing a clear writing style, with suggestions for clear writing, words and structures to avoid as well as a section on alternatives for the ambiguous words and phrases that appear in police writing.

Answers

Exercise 1.1

Read the following police narrative to find answers to the above questions:

On 10-08-14, at approximately 1915 hrs, I was dispatched to 14
Sycamore Avenue, New Town, following a call from a concerned neighbour (Marie Pritchard) about a domestic dispute.

Upon arrival I determined that an argument had took place between John Davis (husband), Jennifer Davis (wife), and George Davis (stepson/son). During the argument in their house, John pulled a knife on George in a threatening manner. George then pulled a baseball bat and struck John.

Paramedics took John to hospital. George was later arrested and charged with assault with a deadly weapon.

Who was involved? -

Marie Pritchard, John Davis, Jennifer Davis, George Davis

What happened?

Following an argument, John pulled a knife on George, who then struck John with a baseball bat

When did it occur?

On 10 September 2014

Where did it take place?

14 Sycamore Ave, New Town

Why was the officer called?

A neighbour had reported the incident

Although the above report answers the questions, it still has gaps. What's missing? After reading the report, what do you not know? Imagine that you are either the CPS or a defense/prosecution barrister. What additional information would you need to prepare for the case?

- The account gives the time of the dispatch but not the time of the incident.
- What was the cause of the argument?
- What did the neighbour witness?
- What was the extent of his injuries

You can probably think of more information needed here.

Exercise 1.2

Read the following report and underline any vague statements.

Several incidents of theft had been reported in relation to the warehousing unit. The *most recent occurrence* that I attended resulted in an injury to an *individual* who needed *medical treatment*. This individual reported being *knocked over* by a person dressed in dark clothing. A witness said that she had heard *a noise* and found the rear doors open and *items* missing.

For further practice, try re-writing the following vague sentences

1.   The suspect stole expensive items from the shop.

John Smith stole two Rolex watches from the shop.

2.   I checked the scene for evidence

As it was raining and windy, I was concerned that evidence might be lost. I walked around the outside of the building and checked the fence. I didn't find anything.

3.   The fire in the house caused substantial damage

The fire at 28 Meadow Drive blew out the windows and destroyed the furniture and carpeting in the living room. Smoke damage was also cause to the walls, floors and appliances in the kitchen.

4.   I proceeded in a northerly direction after the suspect.

At the junction of Rightington Street and the High Street, I turned left and followed the suspect in the direction of St Peter's Church. (in your own communications you may use compass directions routinely, but remember that most people do not know which direction north is so for clarity, you might need to explain in everyday terms)

Chapter 2

The Basics

Objectives

By the end of the chapter you will be able to:

- demonstrate an understanding of parts of speech and their role in sentences
- construct verbs using a variety of tenses
- be able to identify sentence elements and understand their role
- write using a variety of sentence types
- write sentences with correct subject/verb agreement
- demonstrate and understanding of the use of active and passive voice
- write with paragraph demarcation that aids clarity and coherence.

Introduction

Grammar is one area that most of us study at school albeit at varying degrees. The teaching of literacy and English language study in schools seems to undergo constant change, with one approach being replaced by another every few years. Consequently, people's learning experiences are inconsistent, with some having learnt strict grammar 'regulations' whilst others followed a more contextualised model where the emphasis was on building writing confidence rather than concentrating on rules.

In addition, we should think of the English language itself as a living entity that is constantly changing, so practices that were frowned upon at school become acceptable and word meanings change. All too often, we learn 'rules' at school that are not rules, rather preferences, for example, 'never start a sentence with a conjunction'. However, we see many instances of this structure in newspapers and literature, such as in William Blake's hymn *Jerusalem:* **'And** did those feet in ancient times'. It is no wonder then, with such mind boggling variation, that many police officers I have talked to have said that they don't feel confident that their writing is as clear and accurate as they would want it to be. This section is aimed at underpinning writing with some of the basic skills that might have been forgotten over time, but which can help in the construction of the complex writing of policing.

A. Parts of speech (word classes)

Parts of speech (or word classes) are the foundation of good writing. It is impossible to begin to construct effective statements and reports, and correct our errors if we cannot confidently identify the role of words in a sentence. Most of us learn at least some of the names related to parts of speech at some point during our school career, but because, having learnt them, we concentrate on simply using them and so we often forget them. Moreover, some of the definitions given to parts of speech in school can be misleading, for example children are often told that a verb is a doing word or an action word, so would find difficulty in identifying the verb 'to be' in the sentence 'I **am** very tired'. You will find the following table a

45

useful point of reference for completing your work on this course

noun	A noun is a naming word. It names a person, place, thing, idea, living creature, quality or action
	Examples include:
	Common nouns which don't begin with a capital letter can be divided into:
	   - **Concrete nouns**: table, ball, dog, bottle
	   - **Abstract nouns**: thought, kindness, arrival
	Proper nouns (begin with capital letters): Paul, London, Prime Minister
	Proper abstract nouns also begin with capital letters: Catholicism, Socialism, Communism

verb	A verb is a word which describes an action or a state . Examples include: walk, talk, think, believe, live, like, want Including modal auxiliary verbs to provide more information about the main verb: You **must** leave now
adjective	An adjective is a word that describes a noun. Examples include: big, yellow, thin, amazing, beautiful, quick, important and can be descriptive, emotive or evaluative Note- an adjective does not always come before the noun: PC Davis was **tired**
adverb	An adverb is a word that usually describes a verb—answers the questions; how, when or where— Examples include: slowly, intelligently, yesterday, well, here, everywhere

pronoun	A pronoun is used instead of a noun, to avoid repeating the noun. Examples include: I, you, he, she, it, we, they
conjunction	A conjunction joins two words, phrases or sentences together. Examples include: but, so, and, because, or
preposition	A preposition usually comes before a noun, pronoun or noun phrase. It joins the noun to some other part of the sentence. Examples include: on, in, by, with, under, through, at
interjection	An interjection often stands alone. Interjections are words that express emotion or surprise, and they are often (but not always) followed by exclamation marks. Examples include: Ouch!, Hello!, Hurray!, Oh no!, Ha! Well
article/ determiner	An article is used to introduce a noun and can be definite or indefinite. Examples: the (definite) a, an (indefinite)

Learning Tip
When thinking about parts of speech we must remember that a word does not belong to any word class until it is in a

sentence, so some words can be used as several parts of speech:

I *thought* I was going to be late. (*thought* is a verb)
That is such a kind *thought*. (*thought* is a noun)

___

Here is a sentence with all the parts of speech labelled:

interjection	pronoun	conjunction	article	adjective
Well,	he	and	the	tall

noun	verb	pronoun	preposition	adverb
man	knocked	her	down	carelessly

Exercise 2.1

Underline the parts of speech asked for in these sentences:

1.   **Nouns**

PC Blake saw the second robber in the car.

2.   **Verbs**

The police officers searched the first three suspects but the fourth escaped.

3.   **Pronouns**

48

Ms Barton said she knew who had stolen her car.

4.   Adverbs

This evening, Deborah walked home quickly because she was terribly scared.

5.   Conjunctions

The patrol car sped through the traffic, so it was first on the scene.

6.   Interjections

The old lady screamed, "Hey! She's stolen my handbag."

7   Adjectives

The drunk driver was trapped in the wrecked car.

8.   Prepositions

The new police officer found the stolen bike on the path near the park gates.

9.   Articles

The bag was empty except for a tissue and an apple.

Exercise 2.2

Label the parts of speech in these sentences:

1.

The	scruffy	robber	jumped	expertly	over	the	fence.

2.

She	ran	into	the	police	station	excitedly.

3.

He	likes	CSI	but	she	prefers	Endeavour

4.

Help!	He	has	taken	my	car.

5.

The	car	chase	ended	speedily	on	a	roundabout.

A word about verbs

Verb Tenses

When we write, we express actions that have happened in the past, the present and those that will happen in the future. However, we often need to talk about actions that happened over a period of time or that were happening at the same time as something else. Verbs, therefore, are very complex; there are more tenses than the simple past, present and future that we are most familiar with. Mistakes in grammar are often the result of not being aware of how to construct verb tenses, often because of the influence of our various dialects. The following section should help raise your awareness of how various tenses are constructed:

PAST TENSES

Simple past

Use for an action that happened at a point in time in the past.

e.g. - I **drove** to the scene this morning.

Past continuous

Use for an action that was happening for a length of time in the past when another action happened in the middle of it.

e.g. - I **was driving** to the scene when my phone rang.

Past perfect

Use for an action that happened in the past before another action in the past.

e.g. - I **had** already **driven** to the scene when my phone rang

Past perfect continuous

Use for an action that had been happening for a length of time in the past up to the moment when another action happened.

e.g. - I **had been driving** to the scene for 30 minutes when my phone rang.

PRESENT TENSES

Simple present

Use when making a general statement of truth at the present point in time.

e.g. - I **drive** to the scene every time.

Present perfect

Use for an action that happened at an unspecified time before the present moment.

e.g. - I **have** already **driven** to the scene.

Present continuous

Use for an action that is happening now.

e.g. - Right now, I **am driving** to the scene.

Present perfect continuous

Use for an action has been happening for a length of time up to the present moment.

e.g. - I **have been driving** to the scene for 30 minutes.

FUTURE TENSES

SIMPLE FUTURE

Use for an action that will happen at a point in time in the future.
e.g. - I **will drive** to the scene later.
OR: I **am going to drive**...

Future continuous

Use for an action that will be happening for a length of time in the future.

e.g. - I **will be driving to the scene** from 9-   9:30.
OR: I **am going to be driving**...

<u>Future perfect</u>

Use for an action that will happen in the future before another action.

e.g. - I **will have** already **driven** to the scene by the time you ring me.

<u>Future perfect continuous</u>

Use for an action that will have been happening in the future for a length of time up to the moment when another action will happen.

e.g. - I **will have been driving** to the scene for 30 minutes by the time I get your phone call.

Of course, you don't need to remember the names of these tenses but knowing that they exist and how they are constructed can help you to correct your own grammar errors, and to explain to others where they might have gone wrong. You can see clearly that the actions that are expressed in these sentences use more than one verb (verb phrases). Errors often appear in one of these parts – *I have driven* (correct) not *I have drove (incorrect)*, for example.

B.   Sentences

Most police officers that I have spoken to, say that they find report writing frustrating. They feel that there is not enough time and the completed task is often not of a satisfactory standard. Comments by supervisors and lawyers would seem to confirm this.

So why do police officers and staff find this task so difficult? The answer does not lie in poor literacy skills but, in part, in the style of writing adopted by the sector. Many police officers have developed a writing style full of long complicated sentences that are difficult to control under time constraints and even more difficult to read.

In this section we will review sentences and their structure and explore how using tighter sentence structure can help produce writing that is effective, accurate and easy to understand. In order to achieve this more easily, I have used technical terms to label sentence elements. You may wonder why knowing this is relevant to your job as a police officer and of course, you have enough to remember without adding such terminology. However, bear with it as you work through this section; once you are clear about the functions of the different parts of a sentence, you can put the terminology to the back of your mind. Those of you who support children with schoolwork should note that they now have to learn all this terminology before they leave primary school to satisfy the New Literacy Curriculum. This reminder here will make you a hero at homework time.

Look at this sentence from a police report:

A quantity of cannabis was recovered from the suspect, which he had tried to conceal by hidden it in his sock.

So what's the problem?

1.   Passive sentence structure (see section D) means that it is not clear who recovered the cannabis. This is an important omission if the case comes to court.
2.   Use of 'hidden' instead of 'hiding'.
3.   The extra information in the second clause (that begins "which...") is out of place. It should come after "cannabis". This makes the sentence clumsy and adds ambiguity.

And the answer?

Try separating the information into two simpler sentences like in this example:

I recovered a quantity of cannabis from James Greenall. He had tried to conceal the cannabis in his sock.

This is a better because:

a)   This first sentence starts with who recovered the cannabis.
b) It includes the name of the suspect.
c)   It has only one fact in each sentence.
d) Each sentence ends with a **full stop**.

Simple, efficient and professional

Because sentences are the building blocks of writing, it is essential to control sentence structure to produce writing that is clear and efficient. To achieve this, you need to think first about what your writing has to do.

Police writing needs to:

- Create a record of an event
- Be unambiguous
- Be read by a variety of people, including   those who have no previous   connection with the criminal justice system, such as jurors
- Be easily understood. For example, lawyers might only have a short time to read a case summary before the court proceedings.
- Be professional

In order to accomplish all this, you will need to use a variety of sentence types. Understanding how sentences work and how they are structured will help you construct your writing effectively

In this section, you will explore how parts of speech are put together to form sentences. As with parts of speech, most people write in their everyday lives using a range of sentences without really thinking about it. However, different sentence types have different functions and features and present a variety of problems. Understanding how to use different types of sentences in your writing helps to avoid some of the most common errors found in police writing: overlong sentences, sentences joined by commas (comma splicing) and lack of agreement between the subject and the verb.

a)   What is a sentence?

This might seem like a pretty basic question but because we are looking at the structures that will help improve the readability of your reports and statements it is important to refresh what you know about sentences.

Simply stated, a sentence is a group of words put together to express a complete thought. It consists of a subject (what or whom the writer is talking about) and a predicate (what the subject is doing or what is happening to the subject). Let's look at how the pieces fit together. It is also an opportunity to look at some of the vocabulary associated with writing that you might have forgotten.

Words

The smallest units carrying meaning that we will need to examine. Look at these examples:

Car/ silver/ sped

As we have seen in section A, each word has a different role in a sentence. In later sections we will look more closely at the effects of choosing particular words.

We put words together to form *phrases*

A phrase is a short, single piece of information:
the silver car

We use phrases to make a *clause*

A clause is a longer group of words that contains more information. It has at least two phrases – a noun phrase (subject) and a verb phrase.

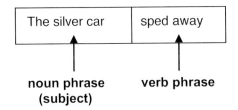

We might join two or more clauses together in a *sentence*.

b) **Identifying independent and dependent clauses**

Because many errors originate from how a sentence is constructed, it is important to be able to identify and understand these two types of clauses. This will help you to correct your own errors and those of others.

An independent clause contains a subject and a predicate and makes complete sense on its own. They can be very short consisting of only one word (a noun) for the subject and one word (a verb) for the predicate. The noun is called the *simple subject*, and the verb is the **simple predicate**.:

He <u>ran</u>

Independent clauses can be long, although they still consist of one subject (a noun and modifiers) and one predicate (a verb and other elements):

The tall, shaven headed ***youth*** with a large spotted dog **laughed** loudly at the young PC's suggestion that he should move along.

Dependent clauses (sometimes called subordinate clauses) also have a subject and a predicate but do not make complete sense on their own. Depending on how it is used in the sentence, they can perform the same action as an adverb, a noun or an adjective:

<pre>
S   V   S   V
</pre>

The mugger ran <u>when   PC James   appeared</u>.

In this example, the dependent clause, underlined, is used as an adverb. The subordinating conjunction *when* introduces a dependent clause that gives more information about (modifies) the **verb** *ran*.

<pre>
S   V   O   V
</pre>

The woman, who <u>is wearing a dark wig</u>, stole the wallet.

This example is a little more complicated. The subordinating word here is 'who', which is also a **relative pronoun**. It is acting as the subject of the dependent clause. The dependent clause describes the subject of the independent clause *woman* and is therefore used as an adjective.

S	V	N

That he is guilty   is stating   the obvious.

In this sentence, the whole independent clause, *That he is guilty*, (an adjectival phrase) acting as the subject of the independent clause. Therefore the phrase is acting as a noun. If this seems confusing try replacing the dependent clause with the word *it* and read the sentence again. You should now be able to see the role of the dependent clause in the sentence.

c) **Sentence types**

The earliest information that you might remember being told about sentences is that a sentence: must begin with a capital letter, end with a full stop/question mark/exclamation mark, contain a subject and a verb and must make sense on its own (in other words an independent clause). The shortest sentence in the English language follows all of these rules:

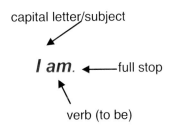

capital letter/subject

I am. ◄——full stop

verb (to be)

i.   Complete sentences

Sentences are the basic whole unit in any writing. There are four main types: simple, compound, complex and compound-complex.

Simple sentences

A simple sentence contains only one independent clause. It should complete a single thought and make sense on its own.

Example:

The speeding motorcyclist was given a warning.

stilted and less interesting, but they can be used effectively in a narrative to highlight certain points or to emphasise the speed of events.

Example:

The fight was in progress when I arrived on scene. Two males, later identified as Barry Griffiths and James Stanley were kicking another male, later identified as Robert Hopkins. As I approached with PC Graham Morley, Barry Griffiths ran away. **James Stanley pulled out a knife. He stabbed Robert Hopkins twice in the chest**. *He attempted to run away but was apprehended by PC Morley.*

If you were the officer attending this scene, you would want to emphasise the speed at which the stabbing took place in order to make it clear that it was unexpected and you were unable to prevent it. The two short sentences in bold achieve this.

Compound sentences

A compound sentence contains two or more independent clauses, usually joined by a co-ordinating conjunction such as for, and, nor, but, or, so (you could use the acronym **FANBOYS** to help you remember).

Example

The robber tried to get away, but PC Mills rugby tackled him to the ground.

Complex sentences

A complex sentence has one independent clause and one or more dependent clauses (remember, a dependent clause does not make sense on its own).

Examples (*dependent clauses* are in italics and the **independent clause** is in bold)

- *If you want the search completed tonight,* **send us more officers**.
- **DI Rogers,** *followed by DS Martin,* **entered the room**
- **PC Morgan,** **the new recruit**, is being mentored by Mike.

As you can see, dependent clauses can be in different positions in the sentence.

Compound-complex sentences

A compound-complex sentence has two or more independent clauses and one or more dependent clauses.

Example

If the suspects turn up, **you go in the front,** *and* **I'll cover the fire exit**.

Unfortunately, errors in sentence construction are frequent in police writing and can lead to a lack of clarity.

Many police officers I have spoken to have said that they have had reports and statements returned to them for rewriting, or that they have been in a supervisory position and have returned an officer's writing because there are errors in sentence structure. In either case they report that although they know that it doesn't 'sound' right, they do not have a clear idea of how it should be corrected. Below are some examples of common mistakes to look out for in your writing.

ii   **Fragments**

A fragment is a group of words that don't make sense on their own. They are often incorrectly punctuated as a sentence.

Examples:

Realising that he had made a mistake. (incorrect)
I realised that he had made a mistake. (correct)
Realising that he had made a mistake, I checked the address myself. (correct)

iii   **Run-on sentences**

Run-on sentences combine two or more independent clauses without punctuation or a conjunction.

Examples:

The car thief broke into the car he drove away towards the tunnel. (incorrect)

The car thief broke into the car. He drove away towards the tunnel. (correct)
The car thief broke into the car, and he drove away towards the tunnel. (correct)*
The car thief broke into the car and drove away towards the tunnel. (correct)**

Note the punctuation in the last two examples:
*   The conjunction joins two independent clauses - a comma is required
**   The conjunction joins an independent clause with a dependent clause - no comma is required.

More examples - A little longer:

A decrease in crime in the area has been attributed to the rise in the number of PCSOs, more than 200 joined the service in the last year alone. (incorrect)

A decrease in crime in the area has been attributed to the rise in the number of PCSOs. More than 200 joined the service in the last year alone. (correct)

Another way of correcting the error in this sentence is to use a semi-colon. A semi colon is used to indicate that although the two clauses are grammatically independent, the ideas are so closely linked they don't warrant separate sentences:

A decrease in crime in the area has been attributed to the rise in the number of PCSOs; more than 200 joined the service in the last year alone. (correct)

Learning tip

Even when correctly punctuated, very long sentences can be very difficult to read and understand clearly. Look at this 102-word sentence from the Association of Chief Police Officers' response to the Government's green paper on policing.

'The promise of reform which the Green Paper heralds holds much for the public and Service alike; local policing, customized to local need with authentic answerability, strengthened accountabilities at force level through reforms to Police Authorities and HMIC, performance management at the service of localities with targets and plans tailored to local needs, the end of centrally engineered one size fits all initiatives, an intelligent approach to cutting red tape through redesign of processes and cultures, a renewed emphasis on strategic development so as to better equip our Service to meet the amorphous challenges of managing cross force harms, risks and opportunities.'

Plain English Campaign, 2009

Sentences like this take so much time and effort to unpick, people just give up. It is much better to use shorter, clearer sentences.

---

iv   Comma spliced sentences

Comma splicing is when two main clauses are incorrectly joined using a comma. This is a common error and can lead to ambiguity.

Examples:

The CSI arrived on scene, she was wearing protective clothing. (incorrect)
The CSI arrived on scene. She was wearing protective clothing. (correct)
The CSI arrived on scene, so she was wearing protective clothing. (correct)
The CSI arrived on scene; she was wearing protective clothing. (correct) *

* When sentences are closely related, they can be joined by a semi colon

---

Learning tip

To proofread for comma splicing, cover all the words on one side of the comma. If the remaining words form an independent clause, cover those words and uncover the words on the other side of the comma. Do they form an independent clause too? If so, you have a comma splice. Correct in one of the ways shown above.

Exercise 2.3

Label the following groups of words as complete (C), fragment (F), run-on (R) or comma spliced (CS).

_____ The suspect escaped.

_____ The burglar broke the window he went into the house.

_____ Start at the beginning.

_____ A teenaged boy, 6ft, dark hair.

_____ The car was searched, it was empty.

Exercise 2.4

Proofread the passage below for fragments, run on sentences and comma splices and rewrite with corrections:

(1) Young offenders in Hindley Prison, Greater Manchester listen carefully, they like the thought of making £200,000 a year legally. (2) Speaking to them is a 33-year-old self made millionaire he knows firsthand about gangs and drugs. (3) Tony

Howard dropped out of school in year ten, he ended up involved with a gang and soon found himself in a Young Offenders Institution however, he eventually learnt how to be a roof tiler. (4) Because he had been in trouble Tony's bosses showed him no respect therefore, he started his own business with a £2,000 loan from his dad. (5) Thirteen years later, he owns two building companies, his business brings in £3 million per year.

d.   Clause elements

So far we have examined the role of words in a text as well as types of sentence and the clauses within them. This provides a good basis for talking about good writing practices in later sections. However, there is one more group of clause elements to mention. These elements are:

subject (S), verb (V), object (O)

It is important to be able to recognise these elements in your sentences because when you are trying to correct an error in a sentence, understanding the relationship between these elements will help you to reformulate it successfully.

The table below offers a summary of these elements and might be useful for your reference.

Clause Element	Description
Subject	The person or thing that does the verb in a sentence and is an essential element. It is a noun or noun phrase, pronoun or dependent clause. • **The suspect** was caught. (noun) • **DC Clarke and DS Barton** went to court. (noun phrase) • **They** want to make a statement. (pronoun) • **What she did** is illegal (dependent clause) Note - the subject is only implied in sentences such as: [you] Stop doing that!
Verb	A verb is another essential element in a sentence. Verbs may be expressed as one word or as a verb phrase. • The mugger **ran** into an alleyway. • PC Dickinson **had been sitting** at the computer all day.

	• Sam **had run** straight into the police officer.
Object	Objects usually follow the verb and can be *direct* or *indirect* and like the subject can be a noun or noun phrase, pronoun or dependent clause. • Direct object - The thief dropped **his crowbar**. • Indirect object - Frank gave **DI Smith** a tip off. * * in this sentence there is also a direct object 'tip off'

As police officers, you will be well aware of the basic structure of investigating a case:

WHO DID WHAT? TO WHOM? WHEN? WHERE? HOW?

You can use this structure when considering clause elements in your writing:

Subject (S) Verb (V) Direct object (DO) Indirect object (IO)

WHO	DID	WHAT
S	V	O
DCI Jacobs	gave	an order

WHO	DID	TO WHOM	WHAT

S	V	IO	DO
DCI Jacobs	gave	DS Maitland	an order

WHO	DID	WHAT	TO WHOM
S	V	DO	IO
DCI Jacobs	gave	an order	To DS Maitland

S	V	Noun predicate
She	is	a police officer
S	**V**	**Adjective predicate**
He	appeared	frightened

Note: Not all verbs need an object

Exercise 2.5

Demonstrate your understanding of clause elements by successfully labelling the subject, verb and object in the following sentences (remember not all verbs take an object). The first one is done for you as an example:

1.

	S	V	O	
Your honour,	Sam Martin	put	the jewellery	into his bag.

2.

73

The jury	went	for lunch.

3.

Henry	had	his window	broken

4.

Sanjid	gave	Mr Fletcher	a ticket.

5.

Marek	went	to the police station

6.

The interview room	is	free

e) Placing Modifiers effectively

In the last section we explored the basic parts of a sentence and their role in successful sentence construction. In this section we will discuss modifiers, which are parts of a sentence that we add on to give more information about a noun or pronoun; they can be a single word or a phrase. It is absolutely essential in police writing that what is written down is accurate. If the modifier is added in the wrong place, errors and ambiguity can occur. Look at the sentence below the modifying phrase is in bold:

PC Richards found a wallet on the desk **that doesn't belong to her**.

This is an example of a common error with modifiers often referred to as *dangling modifiers*. The writer probably thinks that he/she is saying that the *wallet* does not belong to PC Richards. What it really says is that the *desk* does not belong to PC Richards. To construct the first meaning, it should be written:

PC Richards found a wallet **that doesn't belong to her** on the desk.

You can see that the modifying phrase '**that doesn't belong to her** 'is now placed close to the noun that it refers to '**wallet**'. It is much more clear and accurate.

Similar problems can occur with the placing of the words 'just' and 'only' in a sentence. Look at the examples below:

Only

The surveillance team watches in the street **only** after dark.
Meaning: not before dark or during the day

The surveillance team watches **only** in the street after dark
Meaning: not in the park or in the office or anywhere else

The surveillance team **only** watches in the street after dark

Meaning: the team doesn't eat, or sing, or dance etc in the street – just watch

Only the surveillance team watches in the street after dark
Meaning: no-one else, just the team watches

Just

The witness **just** told DS Edwards what she had seen.
Meaning: The witness recently told DS Edwards

The witness told **just** DS Edwards what she had seen.
Meaning: The witness told only DS Edwards

The witness told DS Edwards **just** what she had seen.
Meaning: The witness told DS Edwards exactly what she had seen

The witness told DS Edwards what she had **just** seen.
Meaning: The witness told DS Edwards what she had recently seen

Worse still, you could introduce absurdity into your writing, which can damage your credibility in court. For example:

The suspect was walking the dog in purple suede cowboy boots.

Having been thrown in the air, I caught the bag of drugs.

The burglar was about 30 years old, stocky, 5′ 10″, with wavy hair weighing about 15 stones

You can see that close attention must be paid to the placement of modifiers to ensure clarity and accuracy. Remember, one phrase that you will never want to utter when giving evidence is : *'what I really meant was ...'*; a moderately skillful barrister will have the jury wondering what other mistakes you have made in your statement.

Learning Tip

To avoid these embarrassing sentence errors, place a modifier as **close as possible** to the word it modifies or describes.

Exercise 2.6

Rewrite these sentences with the modifier correctly placed for clarity and accuracy.

1.   The DCC reads from the prepared statement wearing glasses.

_____

2.   As we begin, I must ask you to banish all preconceptions about the case from your mind, if you have any.

_____

_____

3.   Many of the councillors congratulated the DCS for his speech at the end of the meeting and promised their support.

_____

_____

4.   PC Turner had driven over with his boss DI Flynn, from their station in a Skoda for the press conference.

_____

_____

5.   Two cars were reported stolen by Greater Manchester Police yesterday.

_____

_____

C. Subject and verb agreement

In the previous sections you have been asked to consider the building blocks of a sentence: clauses, sentence elements and modifying phrases. In this section, we will concentrate on how to make the subject and verb agree in a sentence.

The simple principle behind subject and verb agreement is: a **singular** subject demands a **singular** verb form:

78

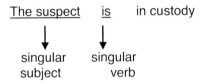

The suspect   is   in custody

singular   singular
subject   verb

A **plural** subject demands a **plural** verb form:

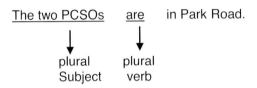

The two PCSOs   are   in Park Road.

plural   plural
Subject   verb

From my experience of delivering language training for professionals, I have noticed that many people find this topic very difficult. This is because most of us do not speak Standard English. Differences in dialect often include subject and verb forms that deviate from Standard English. For example, in some parts of the country, you might hear: 'We was just looking', whilst in others a person might say: 'I were just looking.' We become so used to hearing and using these incorrect forms that sometimes the correct version 'just doesn't sound right', or actually sounds less formal. Added to this confusion is the fact that some subjects appear to be plural, but take a singular verb form:

Everyone involved in the case is asked to attend a briefing at 1600hrs.

The jury is taking a break.

In police writing, the problem can be increased because of a writer's preference for long sentences. In these sentences, information might be inserted between the subject and the verb so that it becomes difficult to maintain correct agreement:

The <u>speech</u> that provoked the demonstrations, prompted the looting and fighting and caused the closing of the city's major roads, <u>was filled</u> with inaccuracies.

As you can see from the examples above, subject and verb agreement is much more complicated than the simple principle suggests. No wonder so many people find it difficult. However, for good professional writing, it is vital to get this right. With this in mind I have included some guidelines that you can refer to in order to ensure correct forms in your writing.

Subject and verb agreement Guidelines (the subject is in bold and the verb is underlined)

1. When the subject of a sentence is composed of two or more nouns or pronouns connected by *and*, use a plural verb.

    She and her friends <u>*are*</u> *giving their statements.*

2. When two or more singular nouns or pronouns are connected by *or* or *nor*, use a singular verb.

The book or *the pen* <u>is</u> on DC Maddison's desk.

*Neither **Sam Bailey** nor **Mike Marshall** <u>was</u> in the vicinity of the crime.*

3.   When a compound subject contains both a singular and a plural noun or pronoun joined by *or* or *nor*, the verb should agree with the part of the subject that is nearer the verb.

The father or **the boys** <u>are guilty</u> of theft.

The boys or **the father** <u>is guilty</u> of theft.

4.   Doesn't is a contraction of does not and should be used only with a singular subject. Don't is a contraction of do not and should be used only with a plural subject. The exception to this rule appears in the case of the first person and second person pronouns I and you. With these pronouns, the contraction don't should be used.

He doesn't <u>like</u> it when he is asked about the theft.

They don't <u>like</u> it when he is asked about the theft.

I don't <u>like</u> *it when he is asked about the theft.*

5.   Do not be misled by a phrase that comes between the subject and the verb. The verb agrees with the subject, not with a noun or pronoun in the phrase.

One *of the security boxes* <u>*is*</u> *open*

The people *who can open a locked door* <u>*are*</u> *few.*

The Chief Superintendent*, as well as his officers,* <u>*is*</u> *anxious.*

The book*, including all the chapters in the first section,* <u>*is*</u> *given in evidence.*

The woman *with all the dogs* <u>*is*</u> *warned by the police officer.*

6.   The words each, each one, either, neither, everyone, everybody, anybody, anyone, nobody, somebody, someone, and no one, seem plural to many people but are singular and require a singular verb.

Each *of these officers* <u>*is*</u> *late.*

Everybody <u>*knows*</u> *Mr Jones.*

Either <u>*is*</u> *correct.*

Don't be confused by phrases, which may contain plural words that come between the subject and the verb:

> *Each* *of the arresting officers* <u>*is*</u> *responsible for writing their own report.*

7.   Nouns such as civics, mathematics, dollars, measles, and news require singular verbs.

> *The news* <u>*is*</u> *on at six.*

Note: the word **pounds** is a special case. When talking about an amount of money, it requires a singular verb, but when referring to the pounds themselves, a plural verb is required.

Five thousand pounds <u>*is*</u> *a lot of money.*

Pounds are *often used instead of Euros in money laundering.*

8.   Nouns such as scissors, tweezers, trousers, and shears require plural verbs. (There are two parts to these things – whoever heard of a trouser?)

These scissors _are_ covered in blood.

Those trousers _are_ to go in an evidence bag.

9.   In sentences beginning with "there is" or "there are," the subject follows the verb. Since "there" is not the subject, the verb agrees with what follows.

There _are_ **many questions**.

There _is_ **a question**.

10.   Collective nouns are words that imply more than one person but that are considered singular and take a singular verb, such as group, team, committee, class, and family.

The team _is briefed_ in the mornings.

The committee _decides_ how to respond to community requests.

The family <u>has</u> *a long history of violence.*

The ambulance crew <u>is preparing</u> *to move in after police clearance.*

11.   Expressions such as with, together with, including, accompanied by, in addition to, or as well do not change the number of the subject. If the subject is singular, the verb is too.

The Chief Constable, accompanied by his wife, <u>is</u> attending the event.

All of the books, including yours, <u>are</u> in that box.

Exercise 2.7

Try these examples putting in the agreeing verb (present tense). If unsure, underlining the subject and the verbs might help:

1.   Gary Dobson _____ going to court.

2.   DI McBride and DCS Barnes _____ at the press conference.

3.   Most of the noise in here _____ caused by people who are intoxicated.

4.   Most of the noises in here _____ caused by people who are intoxicated.

5.   A stock of new notebooks _____ been ordered.

6.   Not one of these officers _____ handed in their reports.

7.   A crowd of onlookers _____ gathered near the scene.

8.   A group of new officers _____ joining the search.

9.   The jury _____ returning a verdict of 'not guilty'.

10   The branches of the service _____ a common goal.

A word about the subjunctive mood.

The English language has four moods. You use most of them all the time but might not be aware of what they are called and by and large you don't need to be:

86

- **the indicative mood** for statements of fact:

  John enjoys practicing at the shooting range.

- **the imperative mood** for commands:

  Watch where you're pointing that gun, John!

- **the interrogative mood** for questions: *How often do you go shooting, John?*

- **the subjunctive mood** for hypothetical and non-factual statements such as wishes, conditions, requests, requirements and suggestions:

  It is advisable that John wear ear protectors when at the shooting range.

As you can see, the subjunctive mood is relevant to our current discussion about subject and verb agreement. Although it is a form that is largely going out of use in everyday speech, it is still important in formal writing.

The most noteable feature of the subjunctive is that it takes the same verb form regardless of whether the subject is singular or plural. If we look at the example above, you might expect to see '*John wears*' not '*John wear*'. In other words, the same verb form is used no matter who is performing the action: *I*, *you*, *he*, *she*, *Mike*, *PC Taylor*, *the sniffer dog*, *we* or *they*.

So when might you use the subjunctive mood? The following examples should form some guidelines for future reference:

1. Statements expressing wishes

These always take *were* –

> *I wish I <u>were</u> back in uniform.*

> *I'll bet DS James wishes he <u>were</u> here with us now.*

> *I wish the suspect <u>weren't</u> so argumentative.*

> *I wish it <u>were</u> the end of this interview.*

> *I wish our team <u>were</u> bigger.*

2. Conditional statements

These often take the form of *If..., then...,* although these words do not actually have to appear in order to express conditionality. Once again, the past tense *were* is used with all nouns and pronouns –

> *If I <u>were</u> in your shoes, (then) I'd interview the suspect myself.*

> *<u>Were</u> I in your shoes, I'd interview the suspect myself.*

If he <u>were</u> my dog, I'd have trained him properly.

If only it <u>were</u> that simple.

I'd have retired years ago <u>were</u> it not for the strength of my team.

3. Requests, requirements and suggestions

These are often expressed with *that* clauses, although the conjunction need only be implied. The rule here is that all nouns and pronouns take the bare infinitive (the uninflected verb form without *to* before it, such as *run, laugh, contemplate* and *work*) –

It's essential (that) <u>she</u> <u>be</u> consulted before you agree to more tests.

I suggest <u>he</u> <u>think</u> things over before deciding whether to continue no commenting.

The doctor recommended <u>PC Smith</u> <u>remain</u> in hospital another week after being hit by the getaway car.

It's crucial that <u>Mary</u> <u>find</u> a solicitor as soon as possible.

It was required that <u>we</u> <u>be</u> at the court two hours before the trial begins.

It's important that the <u>van</u> <u>be</u> searched thoroughly.

You will have noticed that many of the subjunctive examples sound rather formal and dated. We are far more likely to express ourselves today in the indicative mood than in the subjunctive:

I suggest he thinks things over.

Rather than

I suggest he think things over.

But in formally written English, such as the minutes of meetings and reports, the subjunctive mood still has a role to play. The subjunctive mood has been included in the New Literacy Curriculum in primary school. So if you support children with homework, this knowledge puts you ahead of some of the teachers.

D.   Active and passive voice

When you write reports or statements, you want your reader to understand clearly **who is doing what to whom**. Look at the two sentences below:

1. DC Blakely questioned the witness.

2. The witness was questioned.

Which one of these sentences is clearer? You would probably choose sentence 1. It states clearly who (DC Blakely) is doing what (questioning) to whom (the witness). This sentence is written in the **active voice**.

Sentence 2 does not make clear who is doing the questioning. This sentence uses the **passive voice**. Using the passive voice could cause problems in a court appearance, which could be months later. What if you have forgotten by then?

So if the active voice is clearer, why is so much of police writing liberally sprinkled with passive constructions? The answer to that question is quite simply, convention. Over the years, police writing has developed a 'house style' or register, which might have been fit for purpose many decades ago but which is now out of line with the needs of modern policing. One of the features of this style is the overuse of the passive voice. Each intake of new recruits adopts this register, so outdated practices continue. However, the active voice is shorter and clearer and this should make up about 80% of your writing.

Active - When the subject of a sentence does the action to the object:

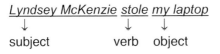

Lyndsey McKenzie stole my laptop
↓   ↓   ↓
subject   verb object

Passive - when we want to emphasis the object or we don't know who did the action:

My laptop   was stolen.
    ↓   ↓
object is   verb
now the
subject

If we know the doer of the action in the passive voice, we put it at the end with 'by' this is called the agent:

My laptop was stolen by Lyndsey McKenzie.

There are times of course when it makes sense to use a passive.

To make something less hostile : 'this fine has not been paid' (passive) is softer than 'you have not paid this fine' (active).

To avoid taking the blame: 'a mistake was made' (passive) rather than 'we made a mistake' (active).

Exercise 2.8

92

Which of the following sentences are active and which passive?

1. The magistrate read the report.
_____

2. The youth didn't deny the charge._____

3. The meeting was called by the community leader._____

4. It was determined by the CPS whether to go to court. _____

5. The officer wrote several reports._____

Change the following passive voice sentences to active voice:

1. Ryan's stolen bicycle was found by PC Lynn Baker.

2. The monthly report was completed by the manager and submitted to the finance officer.

3. It was determined by the police that the burglars had entered through the side door of the centre.

4. The DI was informed by PC Hunter, that Gina's room had been searched.

We will look at active and passive voices in the context of police writing when we discuss writing style later in the book.

E.   Writing in paragraphs

In the previous sections we have seen how to construct different types of sentences and how grammar works within them. However, most police reports are also divided into a number of paragraphs and many people are unsure where to end and begin these units of writing. Clear paragraph demarcation gives structure and coherence to your writing and makes it clearer for the reader. If you are unsure how to structure paragraphs effectively, the following points might help you:

- o   Good paragraphs divide your writing up into major points or events.

- o   Each paragraph should cover only one topic and your reader should be able to understand what each paragraph is about. To remember when to change to a new paragraph, the following acronym should help

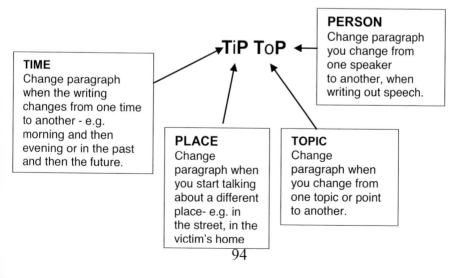

PERSON
Change paragraph you change from one speaker to another, when writing out speech.

TiP ToP

TIME
Change paragraph when the writing changes from one time to another - e.g. morning and then evening or in the past and then the future.

PLACE
Change paragraph when you start talking about a different place- e.g. in the street, in the victim's home

TOPIC
Change paragraph when you change from one topic or point to another.

- Paragraphs often start with a topic sentence or part of a sentence – a statement which is expanded on in the rest of the paragraph. (Try reading only the first sentence of each paragraph of a long work related communication. You can get a flavour of the key points for the whole text and makes reading quicker and more effective.)
- The topic sentence acts as a 'signpost' directing your reader through the report/narrative, making your writing clearer and easier to follow.

Exercise 2.9

Where would you divide the following extract into paragraphs?

More needs to be done to strengthen training for officers around stop and search legislation, says Paul Ford, secretary of the Police Federation National Detectives' Forum. The Federation's call for more training came in response to the recent Stop and Search Powers 2 report, published by HMIC last month, which stated that the police service fails to understand the impact of stop and search, particularly on young people and those from black and ethnic minority communities. Mr Ford said that cuts are impacting on frontline services, and more training is needed to bolster understanding of legislation and the way stops are carried out. He added: "The issues surrounding stop and search are complex, and it does not come as a surprise that this report has recognised the lack of scrutiny from front line supervisors, as they are struggling to cope with budget cuts which have severely affected officer numbers.

(Police magazine, April 2015)

Conclusion

In this chapter we have refreshed knowledge of the basics of grammar and of some of the terms associated with the topic. Of course, we don't need to know lots of linguistic terminology to carry out everyday writing tasks effectively but for the purpose of developing more effective writing skills, it is helpful to know how the nuts and bolts of the language fit together.

When I was learning to drive many years ago. I found it very difficult to gain clutch control so was constantly kangaroo jumping down the road. I asked my instructor to explain what the clutch did and how it worked. He drew me a diagram and explained in detail what happened when I put my foot on the clutch and what changing gear did to the engine etc. Because I could visualise and understand how all the parts worked together, I quickly gained control and my driving became more proficient. In the same way, understanding how language works helps in taking control of your writing, enabling you to produce high quality, professional texts more efficiently.

Remember, if English is your first language, you already know most of the grammar you need; if it isn't, you probably know more about grammar than the average native English speaker. In your writing, you don't need to focus on all the little rules; if you worry about it too much, you will never write anything. The advice throughout this book is to focus on what the reader needs to know, write it as clearly as possible and use the information in this chapter to check on any points of grammar you are not sure about.

Answers

Exercise 2.1

Underline the parts of speech asked for in these sentences:

1.   Nouns

PC Blake saw the second Robber in the car.

2.   Verbs

The police officers searched the first three suspects but the fourth escaped.

3.   Pronouns

Ms Barton said she knew who had stolen her car.

4.   Adverbs

This evening, Deborah walked home quickly because she was terribly scared.

5.   Conjunctions

The patrol car sped through the traffic, so it was first on the scene.

6.   Interjections

The old lady screamed, "Hey! She's stolen my handbag."

7   Adjectives

The <u>drunk</u> driver was trapped in the <u>wrecked</u> car.

8.   Prepositions

The new police officer found the stolen bike <u>on</u> the path <u>near</u> the park gates.

9.   Articles

<u>The</u> bag was empty except for <u>a</u> tissue and <u>an</u> apple.

Exercise 2.2

Label the parts of speech in these sentences:

1.

article	adj	noun	verb	adverb	prep	article	noun
The	scruffy	robber	jumped	expertly	over	the	fence.

2.

pronoun	verb	prep	article	adjective*	noun*	adverb
She	ran	into	the	police	station	excitedly.

* In the example above *police* describes *station* but over time they have become a single unit. If you have written noun across the two boxes, that is acceptable.

pronoun	verb	noun	conj	pronoun	verb	noun
He	likes	CSI	but	she	prefers	Endeavour

3.

4.

interjection	pronoun	verb	verb	pronoun	noun
Help!	He	has	taken	my	car.

5.

article	adj*	noun	verb	adverb	prep	article	noun
The	car	chase	ended	speedily	on	a	roundabout.

* Here *car* describes the *chase* so in this example is an adjective not a noun

Exercise 2.3

Label the following groups of words as complete (C), fragment (F), run-on (R) or comma spliced (CS).

____C_____ The suspect escaped.

____R_____ The burglar broke the window he went into the house.

____C_____ Start at the beginning.

____F_____ A teenaged boy, 6ft, dark hair.

____CS_____ The car was searched, it was empty.

Exercise 2.4

Here is a suggested correction for the passage. You might have written something different

(1) Young offenders in Hindley Prison, Greater Manchester listen carefully; they like the thought of making £200,000 a year legally. (2) Speaking to them is a 33-year-old self made millionaire who knows firsthand about gangs and drugs. (3) Tony Howard dropped out of school in year ten. He ended up involved with a gang and soon found himself in a Young Offenders Institution. However, he eventually learnt how to be a roof tiler. (4) Because he had been in trouble, Tony's bosses showed him no respect. Therefore, he started his own business with a £2,000 loan from his dad. (5) Thirteen years later, he owns two building companies. His business brings in £3 million per year.

Exercise 2.5

1.

	S	V	O (direct)	
Your honour,	Sam Martin	put	the jewellery	into his bag.

2.

S	V	
The jury	went	for lunch.

101

3.

S	V	O	
Henry	had	his window	broken

4.

S	V	O (indirect)	O (direct)
Sanjid	gave	Mr Fletcher	a ticket.

5.

S	V	
Marek	went	to the police station

6.

S	V	
The interview room	is	free

Exercise 2.6

Rewrite these sentences with the modifier correctly placed for clarity and accuracy.

1.   The DCC, wearing glasses, reads from the prepared statement.

2.	As we begin, I must ask you to banish all preconceptions about the case, if you have any, from your mind.

3.	At the end of the meeting, many of the councillors congratulated the DCS for his speech and promised their support.

4.	PC Turner, with his boss DI Flynn, had driven over in a Skoda from their station for the press conference.

5.	Greater Manchester Police reported that two cars were stolen yesterday.

Or

	Yesterday, Greater Manchester Police reported that two cars were stolen.

Exercise 2.7

1. Gary Dobson __is_____ going to court.

2. DI McBride and DCS Barnes ___are_____ at the press conference.

3.   Most of the noise in here ___is___ caused by people who are intoxicated.

4.   Most of the noises in here ___are___ caused by people who are intoxicated

5.   A stock of new notebooks _has___ been ordered.

6.   Not one of these officers ___has___ handed in their reports.

7.   A crowd of onlookers ___has___ gathered near the scene.

8.   A group of new officers ___is___ joining the search.

9.   The jury __is___ returning a verdict of 'not guilty'.

10   The branches of the service ___have___ a common goal.

Exercise 2.8

Which of the following sentences are active and which passive?

1. The magistrate read the report. _____Active_____

2. The youth didn't deny the charge.____Active_____

3. The meeting was called by the community leader._____Passive___

4. It was determined by the CPS whether to go to court. _Passive_

5. The officer wrote several reports.____Active_____

Change the following passive voice sentences to active voice:

1. Ryan's stolen bicycle was found by PC Lynn Baker.

   PC Lynn Baker found Ryan's stolen bicycle.

2. The monthly report was completed by the manager and submitted to the finance officer.

   The manager completed the monthly report and submitted it to the finance officer.

3. It was determined by the police that the burglars had entered through the side door of the centre.

   The police determined that the burglars had entered through the side door of the centre.

105

4.   The DI was informed by PC Hunter, that Gina's room had been searched.

PC Hunter informed the DI that Gina's room had been *searched.*

Exercise 2.9

More needs to be done to strengthen training for officers around stop and search legislation, says Paul Ford, secretary of the Police Federation National Detectives' Forum.

The Federation's call for more training came in response to the recent Stop and Search Powers 2 report, published by HMIC last month, which stated that the police service fails to understand the impact of stop and search, particularly on young people and those from black and ethnic minority communities.

Mr Ford said that cuts are impacting on frontline services, and more training is needed to bolster understanding of legislation and the way stops are carried out. He added: "The issues surrounding stop and search are complex, and it does not come as a surprise that this report has recognised the lack of scrutiny from front line supervisors, as they are struggling to cope with budget cuts which have severely affected officer numbers.

Chapter 3.

The mechanics of language – Punctuation

Objectives

By the end of the chapter you will be able to:

- demonstrate an understanding of the role of punctuation in constructing meaning.
- correctly punctuate sentences
- use commas in a variety of functions
- use apostrophes for contraction and possession
- employ a range of punctuation to enhance and clarify writing

Introduction

When we communicate with another person, we have to consider what is meant: was a threat made, did a person intend to cause offence to someone, did someone make a joke. In a spoken interaction this is easier; we use body language, intonation, pauses, gestures and facial expressions to help the addressee understand what we are intending to say. Consider intonation in the examples below:

I didn't say you stole my purse. (Someone else did)
I *didn't* say you stole my purse.(I said something else)
I didn't *say* you stole my purse. (I just thought it)
I didn't say *you* stole my purse. (I said someone else stole it)
I didn't say you *stole* my purse. (Maybe borrowed it)

I didn't say you stole *my* purse. (I said you stole someone else's)

I didn't say you stole my *purse*. (I said you stole something else)

As you can see all the utterances above have the same words but the emphasis on different words in each one results in a different meaning. In writing, however, we have to find another way of signalling to our reader what we mean to say and how we mean to say it. To do this we have to rely on punctuation to carry all of these aspects of meaning.

If we think of the role of punctuation in this way when we write, rather than as a set of rules that we learnt to one extent or another at school, it makes more sense. This allows you to make more effective choices, guaranteeing the clarity of your writing. Ineffective choices can confuse the reader and make your meaning unclear. Consider these two sentences:

Mike Bradley said the police officer was dishonest. (here the police officer is dishonest)
Mike Bradley, said the police officer, is dishonest. (here Mike is dishonest)

We can see from these short examples that a variation in commas results in an opposite meaning. When a person writes, they often concentrate on the words and not the punctuation, believing that they have expressed one thing, when in reality the meaning is very different. Should these texts become part of the legal process as in the case of your writing, such mistakes can be catastrophic. In addition, there are times when police writing has to be read aloud by someone else in court. It is vital that you have conveyed the events as accurately and clearly as possible.

In order to illustrate this, the following case study is an example of the kind of misunderstanding that can happen as a result of misplaced punctuation.

Case study

The Two Million Dollar Comma

Canadian cable TV company, Rogers Communications, wanted to hire space on pylons, managed by Aliant Inc, to carry their cables to homes across Canada. They agreed what they thought was a five year, fixed fee contract. However, Aliant gave one year's notice of their intention to end the agreement a year early. This would result in Rogers having to pay an extra cost of over $2 million

The dispute centred on the following single clause:

*"[…This Agreement] shall be effective from the date it is made and shall continue in force for a period of five years from the date it is made, **and thereafter for successive five year terms**, unless and until terminated by one year prior notice in writing by either party."*

Aliant argued that according to the rules of punctuation, the second comma closed the dependent clause, 'and thereafter for successive five year terms'. This means that the subsequent qualifier ' unless and until...etc' completed the independent clause. Therefore the right to cancel did not exclude the first five years.

Explanation

To explain let us examine a simpler sentence:

The lawyer drafted the agreement.

This is a complete sentence that makes sense on its own. If we wanted to add some information that wasn't essential to the meaning of the sentence, we have already seen that we can add a dependent clause in the middle of the sentence:

The lawyer, **who worked for Rogers**, *drafted the agreement.*

You can see if you remove the dependent clause in bold, the original sentence remains. If you reread the Rogers/Aliant agreement, you can see that it follows the same structure.

the court in this case agreed with Aliant and ordered Rogers to pay the amount owing.

This chapter aims to remind you, not only of some of the basic rules of punctuation but more importantly, how to use it to convey your meaning clearly. Remember, you shouldn't over punctuate your sentences, just choose the punctuation that makes your meaning clear.

A   Capitalisation

Capital letters are used for two main purposes in English

- To show the start of a sentence
- To show that a noun is a proper noun

The latter can include the following:

- names of people or pets (June Davis, Skip)
- Places (London, Liverpool, France)
- languages (English, German)
- religions or belief system (Christianity, Communism, Judaism
- days of the week and months of the year, *but not seasons* (Thursday, March),
- family relationships if used instead of a name ('I asked **Dad** if I could go' *but not* 'I asked **my dad** if I could go')
- The pronoun *I* is always capitalised

B.   Commas

Commas are not just annoying marks on the paper, which can be used at random or omitted altogether. Commas can help your reader to understand which is the most important information and which is secondary. This is particularly important in policing where information needs to be understood quickly. Often, when I ask students on my courses what they know about commas, they will say they mark a pause or when you need to take a breath. This works sometimes, but the reality is, when officers are carrying out writing tasks in a busy office, there might be any number of interruptions; the phone or a query from a colleague. All of this makes those guidelines difficult to follow. The result is often so many commas that a reader following the same guidelines would begin to hyperventilate.

111

There are basically four main reasons for using a comma:

1a.   To separate an introductory dependent clause or phrase from the main clause in the sentence. They can be quite short like this example:

After the briefing, DC Morris set about his task of checking the suppliers of green nylon rope.

or much longer as in this example:

Whilst most of the officers were searching the wooded area, PC Smith and PC Peters were sent to search the neighbouring field.

If we look at this construction more closely, we can see that the comma gives the reader a pause. This signals the beginning of the part of the sentence that has the subject. Remember, the subject tells your reader what or whom the sentence is about. A comma assists your reader focus on the most important part of the sentence, helping them to process the information more effectively.

Learning tip

If the dependent clause is very short, you can omit the comma unless this causes confusion:

Nationwide there has been an increase in knife crime.

Nationwide, police officers are tackling more knife crime.

In the first example it is clear that *nationwide* refers to *knife crime*. In the second example it would be unclear whether *nationwide* referred to *police officers* or *knife crime*. The comma makes it less ambiguous.

---

b. If the independent clause comes at the beginning of a sentence, it is not necessary to separate them with a comma except where the dependent clause is not essential to the meaning of the sentence. Look at the examples below:

The witness was ready to leave when the SIO arrived.

This means that the witness, who was waiting for the SIO's arrival, could only leave when he/she arrived

The witness was ready to leave, when the SIO arrived.

Here, the witness was leaving. The SIO just happened to arrive at that time.

2. Use commas to separate independent clauses when they are joined by any of these seven coordinating conjunctions: *and, but, for, or, nor, so, yet.*

The body had been removed, but the crowd refused to move away.

The briefing was early in the morning, so DCI Williams brought in some pastries and muffins for the team.

3. Use a pair of commas in the middle of a sentence to separate clauses, phrases, and words that are not essential to the meaning of the sentence. Use one comma before to indicate the beginning of the clause, and one at the end to indicate the end of the clause.

If you are unsure you can ask yourself:

- If you leave out the clause, phrase, or word, does the sentence still make sense?
- Does the clause, phrase, or word interrupt the flow of words in the original sentence?
- If you move the element to a different position in the sentence, does the sentence still make sense?

If you answer "yes" to one or more of these questions, then the element in question is nonessential and should be set off with commas. Here are some example sentences with nonessential elements:

Clause: *The suspect,* **who was wearing a dark coloured jacket**, *was seen running away from the car park.*

Phrase: *Being a police officer out on the street is very interesting. The paperwork,* **on the other hand**, *is a nightmare.*

114

Word: *I appreciate your hard work on this case. Today, **however**, we have charged someone for the thefts.*

4.   Use commas to separate items in a list

The thief took the money, two lamps and a laptop.

You will notice that there is no comma in front of the 'and' at the end of this list, and most people remember this rule and will stick to it without checking that the meaning is clear. Police officers often have to include lists in their statements so it is worth reexamining this as sometimes following this rule leads to confusion. Look at the sentences below:

The young PC thanked his parents, the Chief Constable and the Police Commissioner for his award.

In this sentence the usual rule of no comma in front of the final 'and' has been followed. In this case, the PC thanks his parents, <u>who are</u> the Chief Constable and the Police Commissioner (2 items). Compare this to the sentence below:

The young PC thanked his parents, the Chief Constable, and the Police Commissioner for his award.

In this sentence the PC thanks his parents and the Chief Constable and the Police commissioner (3 items). Either version is punctuated correctly; it all

115

depends on the meaning. In this case, the placing of the comma was a choice to select the correct meaning. Sometimes, the correct meaning is impossible to extract without including a comma before the last item:

The officers sent out for three sandwiches: tuna, ham and cheese and salad.

According to the usual rule, this sentence is correctly punctuated, but what were the three sandwiches they ordered? Was it (1) tuna (2) ham and cheese (3) salad **or** was it (1) tuna (2) ham (3) cheese and salad? It is impossible to tell. You would need to insert a comma before one of the 'ands' for clarity.

This type of comma is called the **Oxford (or Harvard) comma**.

The list below adds some other specific uses of commas for your reference.

- **Before direct speech.**

  The Judge said, "You must answer the question."

- **Direct address** – you use commas to separate nouns of direct address

DI McCreedy, have you interviewed the suspect?

- **Contrasted sentence elements** –

He is ill, not drunk.

- **For clarity** – You can use a comma to separate any elements of a sentence that might be confused or misunderstood.

Where she was, was no concern of mine.

Learning tip

'Which' or 'that' clauses

When you are typing a report using 'WORD' or a similar word processing system, you might have noticed a green line under 'which' or 'that' in a sentence. These two words are often used interchangeably but this is incorrect, They need specific punctuation and have different meanings.

Commas are generally used with "which" clauses but not with "that" clauses.

The word, "which" usually indicates a phrase that provides additional information but does not restrict or limit the object, it modifies.

The notebooks, which are black, are new.

(All of the books are new – they are all black.)

The word "that" usually indicates a clause that provides essential information
restricting or limiting the object it modifies, also known as a "restrictive" clause.

The notebooks that are black are new.

(Only the black books are new.)

Exercise 3.1

Insert commas and capital letters where necessary in the following sentences:

1.   the officer saw them slide scramble and tumble down the embankment.

2.   jack the ripper the infamous criminal was never arrested.

3.   jim and barry found the injured boy so they phoned for help.

4.   gentlemen this is dave richards the new di.

5.   the young pc shouted "he is coming down the stairs. Stop him!"

6.   if you want to protect yourself when out on the streets you must wear your stab vest at all times.

7.   because of its importance to the ultimate outcome of the investigation the first hour of a criminal enquiry is commonly known as the "golden hour".

8.   the police and criminal evidence act 1984 requires the use of pocket notebooks to record evidence in particular circumstances so officers are reminded that these entries form part of the evidence in a case.

C.   Apostrophes

1.   The apostrophe is used to show that a letter, or letters, has been missed out.

    Example:

    Do not = don't   it is = it's   I shall = I'll

    they have = they've

Note – the apostrophe is placed where the missing letters should be.

Learning tip

Many people get confused with *its* and *it's*.

Remember if you are not saying *it is* – you don't need an apostrophe.

---

2.   The apostrophe is used to show possession, that something belongs to someone or something else. In this case, think of the apostrophe as a mark that means 'of'.

To show a single possessor the apostrophe comes before the s.

Peter's car.

To show more than one possessor the apostrophe comes after the s.

The drivers' cars.

The boy's bike = one boy possesses the bike / the bike of the boy

The boy's bikes = one boy owning more than one bike / the bikes of the boy.

The boys' bike = more than one boy share one bike / the bike of the boys.

The boys' bikes = several boys each have a bike / the bikes of the boys

Some exceptions

If the single noun (which is doing the possessing) already ends in the letter 's', then the apostrophe will come after this 's', with or without a further 's':

e.g. *the dress' material, Charles's   grandmother.*

While most nouns become plural by adding an 's', there are others which   change their lettering instead.

e.g. 'man' becomes 'men', 'child' becomes 'children', 'baby' becomes 'babies'.

Here, the plural noun takes apostrophe and 's', unless the plural ends in an 's' already, in which case add only an apostrophe.

e.g.

the man's shoes → *the men's shoes*

the child's swing → *the children's swing*

the baby's mittens → *the babies' mittens.*

Remember – write the whole word for the possessor ie man/men, dog/dogs, lady/ladies, then add the apostrophe, then decide whether an 's' is also needed.

Learning tip

If you understand the use of an apostrophe for contractions but get confused about where to put the apostrophe to show possession, you might find it easier to think of it like this – **there is only one rule: contraction**.

To illustrate this idea, we need to look back in history to the 14th Century and the writing of Chaucer. In his book The Canterbury Tales, he wrote about various people on a pilgrimage to Canterbury Cathedral using a form of language called Middle English. One of these stories was:

122

The Knyghtes tale (The Knight's Tale)

In Middle English an inflection (extra letters) was added to the word knyght to show possession. Here we have es added to knyght to show that it is the tale *of* the knyght. As time passed, we changed the spelling to knight and stopped using inflections to show possession. Instead, we **contracted** it, using **'s** instead of the **es**. This leaves the modern form **knight's**.

However, we still have an inflection in modern English; the practice of adding **s, es or ies** to the end of most nouns to make them plural. When combined with the **'s** to show possession, it becomes rather awkward: knights's, dogs's or worse still, houses's or foxes's. The answer is to contract further and remove the **s**. Now we have knights' swords, dogs' biscuits, houses' gardens, foxes' cubs. If you don't add **s, es or ies** to make the plural in words such as men, women and children, you don't need to drop the s, as shown in the examples above.

Hopefully, if this was something you found confusing, understanding how we came to use the apostrophe for possession might help.

Adapted from dreaded-apostrophe.com

Exercise 3.2

Insert apostrophes in the sentences below. There may be more than one possible answer.

1. The hostages survival depends on her staying quiet.

2. The Human Resources Department is concerned with the employees legal rights, their developmental needs, and also their line managers annual appraisal.

3. Special Constables have been recruited through advertisements placed on the forces website.

4. The Lord Mayors chains disappearance was of interest to the countys police force who were pursuing investigations into various thefts in the towns central business district.

5. The companys accounts listed only the main costs incurred throughout that years operations.

D.   Ellipsis

Like the apostrophe, an ellipsis is used to indicate missing features, in this case, words rather than letters. It is formed using three full stops with spaces between them (...) and are used:

- to show an omission of a word or words (including whole sentences) from a text, usually because they are not relevant.
- to create a pause for effect.

- to show an unfinished thought.
- to show a trail off into silence.

Note: It is also possible to use a dash to create a pause for effect

However, police writing rarely needs an ellipsis because only relevant material should be included and none of the other uses above apply to this form of writing. Problems can arise when officers use ellipsis instead of other punctuation.

Example

Left Jones Brothers Haulage at 1800hrs . . . Interviewed Brian McEwan . . . Had no recollection of incident . . . Radioed details of missing equipment . . . Pending further investigation . . .

E.   Colons and semi colons

a.   You use **colons** for the following:

- after a statement introducing a list
- before an explanation of a statement:

  Community engagement serves two purposes: it benefits the local community and the police officers who serve there.

- to introduce a formal quotation:

The Chief Constable began his talk by saying: "It is a great pleasure to be here tonight."

There is a tendency, in police writing, to overuse the colon. For example, a heading does not always need a colon following it.

Example:

PLAN OF ACTION

XXXXXXXXXXXXXXXXXXXXXXXXXXXXXXXX

XXXXXXXXXXXXXXXXXXXXXXXXXXXXXXXX

You **would** need a colon if the body of writing continued on the same line and space is limited.

PLAN OF ACTION: XXXXXXXXXXXXXXXXX

XXXXXXXXXXXXXXXXXXXXXXXXXXXXXXXX

b.   You use **semi-colons** for the following:

- to join two independent clauses: *The Judge entered the courtroom; everyone stood up.*

- to separate elements in a series when there are commas in the clauses: *PC Smith has arrested Bill Bradshaw, a burglar; Marie Evans, a prostitute; and Janet Fisher, a pickpocket.* If commas also separated the elements it would be difficult to see whether PC Smith had arrested three or six people. In police writing this is usually clearer given in a list format.

- before conjunctive adverbs such as 'however', 'therefore' and 'nevertheless' when connecting two independent clauses: *The suspect tried to get rid of the knife; however, DS Amy Martin found it under a bin* (note the comma **after** the conjunctive adverb).

F   Quotation marks '. . .'

Quotation marks, sometimes referred to as speech marks or inverted commas, can be used singly or doubly. In the UK, the preference is for single quotation marks as above, whereas in the US the double mark is always used. Today however, both forms are acceptable, as long as you are consistent with their use. There are a number of uses for quotation marks including: direct speech, drawing attention to a particular word, reproduced text, titles or to express irony. Because police officers often have to write down the words of others, This is the usage you will be most familiar with. It is important, for clarity, to punctuate correctly.

a.   Direct quotation:

The suspect said, 'I don't know what you are talking about.'

Note, the quotation mark after the comma introducing speech and after the full stop/question mark/exclamation mark. The quotation starts with a capital letter. This will be correct most of the time but you might have exceptions such as the following:

Do you think he was telling the truth when he exclaimed, 'I don't know what you are talking about!'?

Here the whole sentence is a question, rather that just the part inside the quotation marks. Therefore the question mark is placed outside the quotation – even if the quotation is also a question:

Do you think he was telling the truth when he exclaimed, 'What are you talking about?'

The sentence above looks awkward but it is the logical punctuation.

Indirect quotation/reported speech does not need quotation marks

He said that he didn't know what I was talking about.

b. **An interrupted quote** – each part of an interrupted quote begins and ends with a quotation mark:

'If you try to hit me again,' said PC Clegg, 'I will have to arrest you.'

c. **A quotation within a quotation** – indicated by double quotation marks (or single if you choose to use double quotation marks generally).

DS Dailey testified: 'During his arrest, the defendant shouted, 'I didn't mean to do it' several times'

d. **Lengthy quotations**

If you have a lot of quoted material, it can be very difficult to read in your narrative of events. One way of writing long quotes is to indent the left margin to write your quoted paragraph. There is no necessity for quotation marks in this format. Similarly, if the quoted material is written in the form of questions and answers there is no need for quotation marks:

Q: *When did you leave work?*

A: *At about 7.30, I had to finish a report*

Q: *What time would you normally leave?*

A: *Between 5 and 5.30.*

e. **Quoting specific words**

We also use single quotation marks to draw attention to a word. We can use quotation marks in this way when we want to question the exact meaning of the word:

I am very suspicious of his 'alibi', I don't think he was with Davies at all.

Learning tip

Take care with the use of quotation marks; they can affect meaning:

During the briefing, DI Molyneux gave 'important' information about the case.

Some writers use quotation marks to emphasise or call attention to certain words or phrases in their writing such as in the sentence above. It succeeds in drawing attention to the word 'important' but it implies that the writer does not agree with the DI's evaluation of the information.

Exercise 3.3

Correctly punctuate these sentences, using quotation marks where necessary. Not all sentences will need them

1.   The probationer is doing well said Sgt Mackie.

130

2.   No the DI said curtly I can't let you have the time off in the middle of an investigation.

3.   My supervisor told me that my spelling is rubbish.

4.   Certainly Mrs Taylor said if he comes back I will let you know.

5.   Did DCI Stanton say who brought in Martin Pierce?

G.   Other punctuation - hyphens, dashes and parentheses

Hyphens (-)   links words, parts of words and numbers: *door-to-door, pro-police, ninety-nine*

Dashes (—)

- in place of 'to': *1998—2010*

- before a summarising statement: *uniformed officers, CID and CSIs —these were all at the scene*

- repeated expression: *she is the suspect — the only suspect at the moment.*

- missing letters for confidentiality: *The message is for DI F —*

- parenthesis: *By Friday — if not sooner — I want your full report on my desk*

Brackets ( )

- around an explanation or aside: *PC Steer (what an appropriate name) is a traffic officer.*

- enclosing the translation of a phrase: *Incidents of TWOCing (taking without owner's consent) is on the rise.*

- sources of information: *The over all crime rate in this area has reduced by 10% (National Crime Statistics)*

Learning Tip

If you carry out some follow on work using resources from the internet, you will sometimes see the term **'parentheses'** used instead of **'brackets'**. Most people use the term 'brackets' so I have used it here, but in fact brackets are square – [ ].

You will have seen the term **'parenthesis'** at the end of the section on 'dashes' above and this might cause some confusion. Parenthesis is a word or phrase that is added to a sentence as an explanation or afterthought. These can be marked off using commas, hyphens or brackets. Look at the following examples:

- *The rain, which had been falling for hours, washed away the evidence.*

- *The rain (which had been falling for hours) washed away the evidence.*

- *The rain - which had been falling for hours - washed away the evidence.*

All of these examples are perfectly correct so which do you choose in your writing? In formal report writing, commas are usually recommended as hyphens and brackets may seem a little informal. However, they can sometimes be used to aid clarity as in the example below:

- *At midnight last night, Sidney Baker (who was only released from prison last week) was caught breaking into a house.*

There is already a comma in this sentence so using brackets is clearer, particularly if the text needs to be read quickly.

If you are supporting children with schoolwork, knowledge of parenthesis is tested as part of the New Literacy Curriculum for primary schools.

Conclusion

In this chapter you have refreshed your knowledge of a range of punctuation. As a police officer, your writing must be clear, unambiguous and professional. Like it or not, people who don't know you, make judgments about you based on your writing. I read a story about a web designer who received an email from a prospective client. The client said that she was going to commission him to design her company's website but noticed that on his home page he had written 'it's' when he meant 'its'.

133

The client said that she thought that this was careless and took her business elsewhere. In the same way, if you have to appear in court, errors and ambiguity caused by inaccurate punctuation will give defence lawyers the opportunity to bring your credibility and professionalism into question.

According to Lynn Truss (Eats, Shoots and Leaves, 2009), 'Punctuation is a courtesy designed to help readers to understand a story without stumbling.' In other words making what you write as easy as possible for your reader to understand. Using the guidance in this chapter will help you to check your own work for errors and if necessary explain to others where they have gone wrong. Remember, punctuation is how we transmit our meaning to our readers and that aim should always be at the forefront of your writing.

Answers

Exercise 3.1

Insert commas and capital letters where necessary in the following sentences:

1. The officer saw them slide, scramble and tumble down the embankment.

2. Jack the Ripper, the infamous criminal, was never arrested.

3. Jim and Barry found the injured boy, so they phoned for help.

4. Gentlemen, this is Dave Richards, the new DI.

5. The young PC shouted, "He is coming down the stairs. Stop him!"

6. If you want to protect yourself when out on the streets, you must wear your stab vest at all times.

7. Because of its importance to the ultimate outcome of the investigation, the first hour of a criminal enquiry is commonly known as the "Golden Hour".

8. The Police and Criminal Evidence Act 1984 requires the use of pocket notebooks to record evidence in particular circumstances, so officers are reminded that these entries form part of the evidence in a case.

Exercise 3.2

Insert apostrophes in the sentences below. There may be more than one possible answer.

1. The hostage's survival depends on her staying quiet.

2. The Human Resources Department is concerned with the employees' legal rights, their developmental needs, and also their line manager's annual appraisal. (managers' if more than one)

3. Special Constables have been recruited through advertisements placed on the force's website.

4. The Lord Mayor's chain's disappearance was of interest to the county's police force who were pursuing investigations into various thefts in the town's central business district.

5. The company's accounts listed only the main costs incurred throughout that years operations.

Exercise 3.3

Correctly punctuate these sentences, using quotation marks where necessary. Not all sentences will need them

1.   "The probationer is doing well," said Sgt Mackie.

2.   "No," the DI said curtly, "I can't let you have the time off in the middle of an investigation."

3.   My supervisor told me that my spelling is rubbish (none needed)

4.   "Certainly," Mrs Taylor said, "If he comes back I will let you know."

5.   Did DCI Stanton say who brought in Martin Pierce? (none needed)

Chapter 4

Spelling

Objectives

By the end of the chapter you will be able to:

- spell words commonly used in your workplace
- use a variety of strategies to aid good spelling
- make correct choices when spelling confusing words
- demonstrate an understanding of spelling rules

Introduction

We have seen in the previous chapters how poor grammar and incorrect punctuation can have a negative impact on the clarity and ultimately, the credibility of police language. Another area of writing in which damaging mistakes can be made is spelling.

No one can claim to be a perfect speller, and when there are time constraints and writing is rushed, we can all make careless mistakes. Most of the time, we can get away with such mistakes because people know what we mean. This is not the case for writing in the criminal justice system. Here, the written word has primacy, so what you actually write must stand. When documents are prepared for court, your report might be reproduced. In this case, your misspelling will be reproduced exactly as you wrote it, with the Latin word [*sic*], which means as written. This practice highlights mistakes made and serves to impeach your credibility as a witness. Remember, people are not born with good spelling skills, nor are they an indicator of intelligence. Unless there is an underlying difficulty such as dyslexia, most people can (with some focussed practice) become confident spellers.

Learning Tip

Don't rely entirely on a spell checker. This will not help you to correct some of the most common spelling errors such as homophones, which we will discuss later in this chapter. If you don't know how to spell something, look it up in a dictionary and then learn the spelling. Take care with online dictionaries. Most of the free ones are American and words might have different spellings or different meanings.

We make different types of spelling errors and can begin to group them in order to explore how to avoid them. These are some of the common problems:

1.   **Careless errors**

This can involve spelling the defendant's details incorrectly or those of other witnesses. It is common to see a name spelt differently in the same report, an error that can lead to claims that the wrong person might be on trial.

Case study

In February of 2012, two police officers visited the house of Sarah Gosling and Ian Hope in response to a report by neighbours of shouting and items being thrown from the windows. Sarah appeared calm and did not make a complaint of assault, so the officers left, warning the couple about littering. Three hours later, Sarah was stabbed to death by her abusive partner. Because of a misspelling of the address in an earlier report of domestic violence the attending officers were not aware of the history of violence and treated the incident as one of anti social behaviour. The IPCC commissioner investigating the incident stated: "Even if the officers had been aware of the domestic abuse history, there was still no reasonable basis to arrest Hope given the circumstances the officers faced." This is undoubtably true, and there was documentary evidence of Northumbra Police being "involved in measures with partner agencies to try to tackle it [domestic abuse in this relationship]." However, the press stressed the error as a failure on the part of police officers and the force's reputation in regard to this case was damaged.

2.   **Misspelling sector specific words**

It is vital to correctly spell words that are common to your sector. Firstly because incorrect spelling of words that you should be using everday gives defence barristers an opportunity to damage your credibility in court. A few years ago, a social worker in one of my classes reported that when giving evidence in a case that she had been working on for some time, The defence barrister pointed out that she had referred to 'The Children's Act', when it should have been 'The Children Act'. The barrister suggested to the jury that if she had made such a basic error, what other errors were in her report. Her credibility as a witness was damaged.

Secondly, learning to spell key words in your sector will help you to reduce writing time. Although using a dictionary is a necessary skill in professional writing, having to stop to look up words that you use every day, slows and disrupts the writing process, and you will probably have to do it again the next time. The common strategy of trying to think of a word that you *can* spell is also time consuming and the alternative word might not be as accurate or effective as the troublesome one.

3.   **Misspelling everyday words**

The most common spelling errors are those of ordinary every day words such as *receive* (my own personal demon) or *occurred.* These words generate questions such as; how many double letters? Do I drop the 'e'? If I add 'ing', do I double the last letter? Most people don't even bother to check their spelling of familiar words, relying instead on that new best friend, the spell checker. Whilst undoubtably a useful tool, spellcheckers will not identify some errors such as 'cloths' when meaning 'clothes'. The following extract from a poem by Jerrold H. Zar illustrates this perfectly:

Eye have a spelling chequer,
It came with my Pea Sea.
It plane lee marks four my revue
Miss Steaks I can knot sea.

(Jerrold H Zar 1992)

The truth is that even a poor speller does not spell thousands of different words incorrectly; errors tend to occurr in groups. As I indicated above, words with 'ie' or 'ei' causes me problems. Some of these spelling difficulties can be resolved by learning a few rules, others by developing strategies to help you remember. These will be discussed later in the chapter.

4.   Confusing words

Lots of 'spelling' errors are not due to incorrect spelling, but from choosing the wrong word due to the complexity of the English language. **Homophones**, for example, are words that sound the same but are spelt differently: *where, were, wear, we're; there, their, they're.* **Homonyms** are words that are spelt the same but pronounced differently: Did you <u>read</u> the book? I <u>read</u> it on my holiday. In addition, there are words that sound similar and are often confused: *affect or effect; all right or alright; alternate or alternative.*

This chapter will concentrate on some of these spelling problems and how to avoid them. If you are not sure what types of words give you problems, you might find the following self assessment useful.

142

Exercise 4.1 - Spelling Self Assessment

Which of these options shows the correct spelling?

1)a. The accomodation in the cells is very basic?

   b. The accommodation in the cells is very basic?

   c. The acommodation in the cells is very basic?

2) a. DC Mitchell's clothes for working undercover were bizaar.

   b. DC Mitchell's clothes for working undercover were bizzar.

   c. DC Mitchell's clothes for working undercover were bizarre.

3) a. The shopkeeper definately saw Morton steal the phone.

   b. The shopkeeper definitly saw Morton steal the phone.

   c. The shopkeeper definitely saw Morton steal the phone.

4) a. It will be necessary for two officers to attend.

   b. It will be neccessary for two officers to attend.

   c. It will be neccesary for two officers to attend.

5) a. PC Bryant will recieve a commendation for his bravery.

b. PC Bryant will rieceve a commendation for his bravery.

c. PC Bryant will receive a commendation for his bravery.

6) a. The vehicle had been statianery for 30 minutes.

b. The vehicle had been stationery for 30 minutes.

c. The vehicle had been stationary for 30 minutes.

7) a. DI Mills will superceed the outgoing Det Supt.

b. DI Mills will supercede the outgoing Det Supt.

c. DI Mills will supersede the outgoing Det Supt.

8) a. Do you think DC Wood will fullfil his early promise?

b. Do you think DC Wood will fulfill his early promise?

c. Do you think DC Wood will fulfil his early promise?

8) a. The patrol car is making a very wierd noise.

b. The patrol car is making a very weard noise.

c. The patrol car is making a very weird noise.

9) a. The officers made the boys hand over they're knives.

b. The officers made the boys hand over their knives.

c. The officers made the boys hand over there knives.

10) a. It is common practise for PCSOs to patrol the estate.

   b. It is common practice for PCSOs to patrol the estate.

   c. It is common practis for PCSOs to patrol the estate.

Developing spelling strategies

It will help you to develop spelling strategies if you have a clear understanding of the 'basic building bricks' that, placed together, form words. It is particularly important to be clear about the difference between 'long' and 'short' vowels. For example:

Short vowel	Long vowel
*a*pple	*a*corn
Short vowel	**Long vowel**
*e*lephant	*e*agle
*i*nsect	*I*sland

a.   vowels and consonants

If you are trying to spell a word you have not seen before, one of the most important clues you have is the sound of the word. The separate sounds that go together to form a word are called *vowels and consonants*

Every word contains at least one vowel sound. In English the vowels are:

a   **e**   **i**   **o**   **u**

The other letters are consonants:

b   c   d   f g h j k l   m n p q r s t v w x y z

Learning Tip

Some spelling problems arise from the sound of the word when we say it in our local accent or when letters used to make the sound are different from what we might expect – for example *photograph* begins and ends with an *f* sound.

Exercise 4.2

Try this – how would you pronounce this word? Check the answers section for an explanation

ghoti

Y : When is it a vowel ? When is it a consonant?

The letter *y* needs some special attention.

It can be either a vowel or a consonant, depending on its function in the word.

Say each group of words aloud and listen to the sound made by the letter *y*:

In these words the letter y makes a consonant sound.	In both these sets the sound of the letter y is a vowel sound.	
yellow yak yoghurt yo-yo.	sky cry fly shy July	twenty baby happy family

Exercise 4.3 - Read the following words and decide if the letter *y* has a vowel sound or a consonant sound. Write **v** or **c** in the box next to the word.

you

sorry

dry

beyond

silly

dynamite ☐

Consonants

Spelling most consonant sounds is usually fairly simple. For example, if you hear the sound /n/ you know to use the letter *n* -*n*ut, lemo*n*, ba*n*a*n*a

However, there are a few which need a closer look. For example:

the /s/ sound is sometimes spelt with the letter *c*, as in circle

the /j/ sound is sometimes spelt with the letter *g*, as in bridge

the /f/ sound is sometimes spelt with the letters *ph*, as in phantom

More spelling mistakes are made with vowels than consonants. This is because:

- each vowel can be used to spell more than one sound
  e.g. d*o*g, g*o*ld
- there are often several ways to spell the same vowel sound
  e.g. r*oa*d, arr*ow*, b*o*n*e*
- two vowels can combine to form yet more sounds
  e.g. d*ow*n, b*oy*, h*ou*se

b   Syllables

SYLLABLES are the number of BEATS in a word. To work out how many syllables in a word, try singing it and see how many notes you need.

For example:

Hap-py   Birth-day   to   you

Happy has two syllables, *Hap - py*, so needs two notes;

Birthday has two syllables, *Birth - day*, so needs two notes;

to and *you* each have only one syllable.

Exercise   4.4
Say each word aloud, count the number of syllables and write it in e.g 3

London	
Singapore	
Manchester	
Australia	
France	
Liverpool	
Glasgow	
Moscow	
Spain	
Argentina	

This can help to work out spellings that you find problematic because you can split the word into syllables and just learn the bits that you find tricky.

c   Prefixes

A *PREFIX* is a syllable added to the front of a word to change its   meaning.
For example:

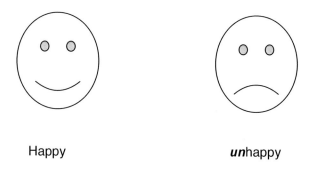

Happy   *un*happy

play > *re*play   like > *dis*like   dose > *over*dose

The original word is called the **Base word** (or sometimes, the *root* word).

Exercise 4.5 - Split the word in column 1 into prefix and base word.

Word	Prefix	Root
replace		
misprint		
unusual		
immoral		
disagree		
subway		
irregular		
prefix		

d.   Suffixes

A *SUFFIX* is a letter or group of letters added to the end of a word to change its meaning. For example:

fly > fly*ing*   help > help*ed*   mist > mist*y*   enjoy > enjoy*ment*

Exercise 4.6 - Split the word in column 1 into base word and suffix.

Word	Root	Suffix
quickly		
thinking		
sweetest		
wonderful		
hopeless		
darken		
cracked		
employer		

Exercise 4.7

Check your knowledge of the main spelling terms: choose the best word to complete each sentence..

The word constable has three...

Select the word here	
	prefix
	suffix
	vowels
	consonants
	syllables
	long
	short

The underlined letters in c**o**nst**a**b**le** are called...

Select the word here	
	prefix
	suffix
	vowels
	consonants
	syllables
	long
	short

The underlined letters in **c**o**nst**able are called...

Select the word here	
	prefix
	suffix
	vowels
	consonants
	syllables
	long
	short

The vowel sound in **chase** is a ___ sound.

Select the word here	
	prefix
	suffix
	vowels
	consonants
	syllables
	long
	short

The vowel sound in **stab** is a ___ sound.

Select the word here	
	prefix
	suffix
	vowels
	consonants
	syllables
	long
	short

The underlined letters in enforce**ment** form the...

Select the word here	
	prefix
	suffix
	vowels
	consonants
	syllables
	long
	short

The underlined letters in **sub**poena form the...

Select the word here	
	prefix
	suffix
	vowels
	consonants
	syllables
	long
	short

Spelling rules

a.   Adding suffixes

Some of the most common spelling errors relate to adding a suffix. Many people are unsure, whether to drop the final 'e' and whether the last letter should be doubled.

Adding a suffix to words ending in a silent 'e'

In most cases, you keep the 'e' if you are adding a consonant suffix e.g. *ly, ment, ful* etc, and drop the 'e' if you are adding a vowel suffix e.g. *ing, ed, able* etc. The table below has some examples:

Base word	+ Consonant suffix		Base word	+ Vowel suffix
hope	hopeless		note	notable
state	statement		late	latest
safe	safely		write	writing
care	careful		manage	manager
aware	awareness		change	changed

This rule applies to most of the words you might want to spell, but of course every rule has its exceptions. These are listed below.

1.   The 'e ' is dropped before a consonant suffix in eight specific words.

whilst   truly   argument   wisdom

duly   wholly   ninth   awful

Learning tip

This sentence will help you to remember them:

Whilst his **wisdom** is now in doubt, **truly** and **duly**, his **ninth argument** is **wholly awful**.

---

2.   Some words have two possible forms before -able.

like - likeable/likable

move - moveable/movable

love - loveable/lovable

3   Words ending in 'ge' keep the 'e' before 'able' to keep the soft 'ge' sound-

157

manageable, changeable, knowledgeable

We also keep the 'e' in words ending in 'ce' before 'able' to keep the soft 'c' ("s") sound-

noticeable, replaceable, serviceable

4.   The final -e is not dropped from words ending in: -ee, -oe,   -ye.

see - seeing, agree - agreeing, canoe - canoeist, dye – dyeing

---

Learning tip

Do take care with some of these words if you are using a spellchecker –

Words such as *dying* and *dyeing* are both correctly spelt but mean different things as does *singing* and *singeing*.

Exercise 4.8

Join suffixes to these base words:

notice + able	
trouble + some	
enforce + ing	
certificate + ion	
impossible + ly	
expire + y	
examine + ation	
expense + ive	
size + able	
courage + ous	

2.   Doubling letters when adding a suffix

Many people I have spoken to say that they have difficulties spelling words with double letters. Whilst there are a number of words that have double letters as part of their internal structure i.e. necessary and accommodation, there are others that sometimes take a double letter when adding a suffix. Learning a few simple rules can help you eliminate some of those double letter spelling problems.

Usually when you add a suffix, the base word stays the same:

> **e.g.** *help + ful = helpful*

But there are several important groups of words where the spelling of the base word **changes** when you add a suffix.

Rule 1

For most short (one syllable) words that end in a <u>single</u> consonant you need to double the last letter when you add a vowel suffix:

e.g. *ru<u>n</u> + ing = ru<u>nn</u>ing fu<u>n</u> + y = fu<u>nn</u>y*

If the word ends with more than one consonant, you *don't* double the last letter:

e.g. *bu<u>mp</u> + ed = bum<u>p</u>ed   bri<u>ng</u> + ing = bri<u>ng</u>ing*

If there are two vowels before the last consonant, you don't double the last letter:

e.g. *sw<u>ee</u>p + ing = swee<u>p</u>ing   l<u>oo</u>t + ed = loo<u>t</u>ed*

Rule 2

For most longer (more than one syllable) words that end in 'l' you need to double the 'l' when you add the suffix:

| **e.g.** | *travel* | + | *ing* | = | *trave**ll**ing* |
| | *cancel* | + | *ed* | = | *cance**ll**ed* |

Take care when using a spellchecker – if yours is set to US spelling it will not pick up this error because the letter is not doubled in US English.

Rule 3

For this rule, you will need to think of how you say the word and where the stress in the word is. For example in the word **BUDjet**, the stress is on the first syllable whilst in the word **adMIT**, the stress is on the second syllable.

For most longer (more than one syllable) words that have the stress on the last syllable when you say them AND end in a single final consonant you need to double the last letter:

> **e.g.** *be<u>gin</u> + er = beginner*
> *pre<u>fer</u> + ing = preferring*

If the word has more than one syllable and ends in a single consonant, but the <u>stress</u> isn't on the last syllable, then you *don't* need to double the last letter before adding a suffix:

> **e.g.** *<u>off</u>er + ing = offering*
> *<u>ben</u>efit + ed = benefited*

Rule 4

If you have a word ending in a consonant and a suffix starting in a consonant, you don't need to double the last letter of the word:

e.g. *enrol + ment = enrolment*

commit + ment = commitment

Exercise 4.9

Add the suffixes 'ed' and 'ing' to the following words commonly used in police reports:

Confer   _____

Occur   _____

Accelerate   _____

Testify   _____

Caution   _____

Witness   _____

Argue   _____

Bribe   _____

Admit   _____

Add the suffix 'able' to the following words commonly used in police reports:

Regret   _____

Approach   _____

Cite   _____

Arrest   _____

Enforce   _____

Add the suffix 'ment' to the following words commonly found in police reports:

Embezzle   _____

Enforce   _____

State   _____

Assess   _____

Judge   _____

Suffixes - problem spellings

Some suffixes and word endings cause problems with spelling because they have the same sound but are spelt differently – e.g. predict*able* but access*ible*; sta*tion* but deci*sion*; techni*cian* but imita*tion*. This section explores these words and offers some guidance of choosing the right ending.

1.   'able' or 'ible'

    Words that end in 'able' or 'ible' are adjectives e.g. arrest*able*, admiss*ible*. The following points should help you to make the right choice.

- If the base word does not change, add '**able**'

understandable	predictable
avoidable	memorable

In some words that end in 'e' or 'y', the word remains the same except the 'e' is dropped or the 'y' is changed to 'i'

e.g. value – valuable   rely – reliable

- Words ending in *'ible'* cannot usually be divided in the same way. When you remove the suffix, you are not left with a complete base word.

> credible   illegible   gullible
> implausible   reprehensible

** Note that *accessible*, *contemptible*, *digestible*, *flexible* and *suggestible* are among the exceptions to this rule

---

Learning tip

There are more words that end in *'able'* (about 1000) than there are in *'ible'* (about 200). The best way to deal with this choice is to learn the common *'ible'* words in your workplace writing and use *'able'* for the others.

---

2.   The 'shun' sound - 'tion', 'sion', 'cian', 'tian', 'cean', 'sian', 'cion', 'shion'

although there are eight different ways to write the 'shun' sound, some of them are quite rare and are used in specific circumstances; for example:

- **cushion** and **fashion** are the only words in standard English that have the '**shion**' ending.

- '**tian'** endings indicate a place of origin or a set of beliefs: **Dalmatian, Egyptian, Christian**

- '**cean'** endings usually relate to the field of science: **ocean, crustacean, testacean**

- **suspicion** and **coercion** are the only two common words that end in '**cion'**

The remaining four are more common but there are ways to help you to remember which ending to choose.

- Words that end in '*tion*' and '*sion*' are nouns, with '*tion*' being the most common: *protection, station, location, condition, communication* are just a few examples.

- Fewer nouns end in '*sion*'. These are usually formed from verbs that end in '*d*', '*de*', '*se*' and '*t*':

  o To collide – *collision*

  o To suspend – *suspension*

  o To explode – *explosion*

  o To decide – *decision*

We can add to those, 'ssion' endings, which are formed in a number of ways:

- o When words end in *'ss'* just add *'ion'* – discuss – *discussion*, confess – *confession*

- o Add 'ssion' to words ending in 'it': permit – *permission*, commit – *commission*

- o Add to words ending *'cede'* or *'ceed'*: concede – *concession*, succeed – *succession*

- Words that end in 'cian' are fewer still and usually refer to occupations:

  - o *technician*

  - o *optician*

  - o *magician*

  - o *statistician*

- Words that end *'cian'* can be used as a noun or an adjective and many of them are uncommon in everyday writing, however some refer to a person's origin and this form is used in police writing:

  - ▪ *Caucasian, Russian, Indonesian*

Exercise 4.10

Add the correct 'shun' endings to the base words in brackets below:

1. PC Golding told the man he had two (opt) _____ , stop shouting or be arrested for disturbing the peace.

2. The evidence was found behind the new radiator in the (extend) _____ .

3. His (react) _____ to the news of his son's arrest was not as bad as I had expected.

4. Traffic was diverted because of a (collide) _____ on the motorway.

5. We had to call out an (electric) _____ to make the building safe before the officers could go in.

6. I get a great feeling of (satisfy) _____ when a crime is solved.

7. I had a (converse) _____ with the DCI about increasing the size of the search team.

b. Adding prefixes

We saw in the last section that suffixes are added to the end of base words. Prefixes are added to the beginning: **post**pone, **tele**phone, **dis**seminate, **pre**meditated. Prefixes often change the meaning of the word.

Understanding the way a word is made up can help with spelling because it can make spelling more logical. We have seen how learning a few rules about adding suffixes can help dispel some of those double letter worries. Similarly, understanding how prefixes are added might further increase confidence. It can also help with working out the meaning of an unfamiliar word. You might find the following points helpful:

- The spelling of a base word does not change when a prefix is added, as in *unwilling.*

- The spelling of the prefix does not change: **contra**dict, **contra**vene, **contra**band

- Double letters can occur, but these are where the last letter of the prefix is the same as the first letter of the base word. If you look at the word ***unnecessary***, there would appear to be a number of problem areas for spellers who struggle with double letters. However, you are adding the prefix ***un*** to the word ***necessary*** (which you should be able to spell with the help of the mnemonic learning aid on pg 202). Understanding the structure of the word will save some agonising over how many letters are doubled. Other examples include

  - **il**legal
  - **ir**responsible
  - **dis**similar
  - **mis**spoke
  - **un**noticeable

- take care – some words contain the same string of letters as a prefix, but they are not prefixes. The *re* in *real* is not a prefix. Other examples include *uncle, pretty, press, interest, reach, irony, dish,* and *antique.*

Adding hyphens with prefixes

There is often some confusion over whether to add a hyphen when adding a prefix. Usually a prefix is added directly to the base word, but occasionally a hyphen is added. There are no hard and fast rules with some words being hyphenated and other words with the same prefix not: *multi*-purpose, *multi*layered. If you are not sure, you should check your dictionary, however, the following guidelines should help.

You should hyphenate:

- when adding the prefix *ex* meaning former

Examples - ex-prime minister, ex-wife, ex-chief constable

(not when meaning out of or away from as in *ex*plosion)

- after the prefix, *self*

Examples - self-sacrifice, self-control

- to separate letter combinations that might cause confusion

Examples: co-opt, de-emphasise, anti-intelligence

(You should note that current style manuals and dictionaries now tend toward "closing" the word (cooperation, reenter) except in cases where readability is affected. Check if your department has a preferred style. If not, pick one but be consistent throughout)

- after the prefix *re* to prevent misreading or confusion with another word.

    Examples:

    Re-cover the evidence when you **re**cover from the shock.

    Please **re**lay the message that they will **re**-lay the carpet after the search.

Understanding how words are formed can be helpful for developing confidence with spelling. When you look a word up in a dictionary, you will not only gain information about the meaning of a word and its spelling; a dictionary can tell you the derivation or origin of a word. You will soon recognise that words belong in families knowledge and understanding of one member will help you to decode or spell less familiar members. Prefixes and suffixes can be features of different word families. Below is a list of the most common prefixes and suffixes but as you come across others, you should note them down for future reference:

Prefix	Meaning	Example
anti-	against	antifreeze
co-	together	coexist
de-	defrost	opposite
dis-	not, opposite of	disagree
en-, em-	cause to	encode, embrace
fore-	before	forecast
in-, im-	in	infield
in-, im-, il-, ir-	not	injustice, impossible illegal, irresponsible
infra-	below, underneath	infrastructure
inter-	between	interact
mid-	middle	midway
mis-	wrongly	misfire
non-	not	nonsense
over -	over	overlook
poly-	many	polygamy

pre-	before	pretrial
re-	return	again
semi-	half	semicircle
sub-	under	submarine
super-	above	superintendent
trans-	across	transport
un-	not	unfriendly
under-	under	undersea

Suffix	Meaning	Example
-able, -ible	can be done	comfortable
-al, -ial	having characteristics of	personal
-ed	past-tense verbs	hopped
-en	made of	wooden, leaden

-er	comparative	higher
-er,	one who	worker, actor
-est	comparative	biggest
-ful	full of	careful
-ic	having characteristics of	linguistic
-ing	verb form/ present participle	running
-ion, -tion, -ation, ition	act, process	occasion, attraction
-ity, -ty	state of	infinity
-ive, -ative, -itive	adjective form of a noun	plaintive
-less	without	fearless
-ly*	characteristic of	quickly
-ment	action or process	enjoyment
-ness	state of, condition of	kindness

-ous, -eous, -ious	possessing the qualities of	joyous
-s, -es	more than one	books, boxes
-y	characterised by	happy

Exercise 4.11

Use a prefix to make the opposite of these words:

1. wrap   _____

2. use   _____

3. agree   _____

4. engage   _____

5. behave   _____

6. understand   _____

7. fold   _____

8. spell   _____

9. connect   _____

10. close   _____

Confusing Words

There are some words in the English language that cause problems, and which your spell checker will not pick up. These are words that come in twos or threes and are confusing because they either sound the same (homophones: *where, were, wear*) or because they sound similar: *accept, except*. Similarly there are some occasions where a writer might be unsure whether a word is just one word or two: *all right or alright*. In my training role, I have seen a number of errors using these confusing words. They can change the meaning of your report and discredit your evidence. In one writing exercise that I marked, an officer reported that a prisoner had been 'taken in to **custardy**'. Imagine how a barrister in a trial might use that error to destroy the credibility of that officer.

In the table below, I have listed the words that my police students have said that they find most difficult. I have given an example to guide you with the correct usage and have added, where possible, a tip to help you remember.

Example	Tip
I can **accept** that you are telling the truth. Everyone **except** DC Jones will be involved in the search.	**EXCEPT = EXCLUDING** Let the first two letters of **ex**cept remind you that it means **ex**cluding.
The cuts will **affect** every department.	Try using the verb *to transform*(in its various forms,

The **effect** of the cuts on the crime rate is disastrous.	e.g., *transforming, transformed, transforms*) instead of *affect*. If the sentence still makes sense, then *affect* is almost certainly correct. However, if you find yourself trying to use *transformation*, then you should be using *effect* because both are nouns. Note – effect is occasionally used as a verb that means to bring in to being: The changes to working hours will be **effected** when agreement is reached with the unions.
I followed my sergeant's **advice** and wrote my report straight away. I would **advise** you to take the sergeant's exam at the next opportunity.	If you can't remember, this sentence might help: **S**end for the **C**at – send is a verb (s) and Cat is a noun (c) This applies to any 'ise' or 'ice' words such as practice/practise; device/devise. ***Note – advised <u>does not</u> mean told** He **advised** me about the changes in the rota. X

The bank employees were **all most** helpful during our search. The mugger **almost** escaped across the park.	Almost means 'not quite or nearly' 'All most' is relatively rare
You will be **allowed** to go after you have signed this form. DS Brennan likes to read his reports **aloud** to check his spelling.	*Allowed* means *permitted* *Aloud* means *out loud.*
The DI is all ready to give the morning briefing. Have you finished working through that list already?	*Ready* can replace *all ready* but not *already*. Try to use just *ready*. If your sentence still makes sense, then you are safe to use *all ready*; otherwise, use *already.* Jean is **all ready**. (Try the substitution: Jean is **ready**. (Therefore, *all ready* is correct.)✓ I have **already** seen the latest play. (Try the substitution: I have **ready** seen the latest play. X (Therefore, *already* is correct.)
PC Kirkby's report was **all right**.	**All right** is always two words. Many people today use **alright** so it is becoming more

All right! Let's start the briefing. It's a puzzle **all right**.	acceptable to use it. However in formal writing it is better to opt for **all right** as using **alright** might be interpreted by your reader as an error – better to err on the safe side.
We found the stolen items **all together** under the shelving. **Altogether** our division has a better clear up rate than the average.	*All together* means *collectively* *Altogether* (adverb) means *with everything considered*.
I **cannot** understand how we missed that piece of evidence	Cannot is always one word.
The DCI **complimented** the team on its success. (verb) The DCI sent his **compliments** to the team on their success. (noun) DS Manley wore a blue tie that **complemented** his new shirt. (verb) DS Manley's tie was an excellent **complement** to his new shirt. (noun)	*Compliment* is associated with praise. *Complement* is associated with enhancement. **REMEMBER:** The word *compliment* has an *i* in it – just like *praise*. The word *complement* has an *e* in it – just like *enhancement*. Note: complement also means composition or make-Do you have a full complement of officers for your search?
We need to **curb** our spending on this investigation.	*To curb* means *to control* or *to limit*.

After the punch, the victim hit his head on the **kerb**.	The word **_kerb_** means _the edging of a pavement. (this word does not exist in US English so take care when using a spell checker)_
We go about a hundred metres **farther** and then turn left into the station car park. We have a **further** 15 arrests to reach our target.	These words are often confused because they can sometimes be interchangeable. Use _farther_ with physical distance Use _further_ with non-physical "distance" If you're unsure which to use because it's difficult to make a distinction between physical and figurative distance, opt for _further_.
The officer found a large quantity of **heroin** under the car seat. PC Nicola Norton was hailed as a **heroine** for rescuing a child from a flooded quarry.	'A **heroine**' is the female protagonist in a film or book. Use gender-neutral '**hero**' when referring to a person of either gender who has carried out an act of bravery.
DI Barton and **I** will lead the inquiry. Do you want to join Steve and **me** on this search?	To check – remove all the other people from the sentence e.g. I will lead the inquiry – it should still make sense. Note – 'between you and me'

	is the correct form <u>not</u> 'between you and I'
The judge has suspended the **inquiry** into the police shooting of the escaped armed robber. I made an **enquiry** about the blue Peugeot that was seen in the vicinity of the robbery.	In the UK, **inquiry** and **enquiry** are interchangeable. However, it is becoming more common to use **inquiry** to denote *an investigation*, and **enquiry** to denote *a question*.
May I see your driving **licence** please? (noun) These premises are not **licensed** to sell alcohol. (verb)	Try using the word *card* (or *papers*) instead of **licence**. If the sentence still makes sense, then **licence** is correct. Try using the verb *to allow* (e.g., *allowing, allowed, allows*) instead of **license**. If the sentence still makes sense, then **license** is correct.
The surveillance team might **lose** the suspect if he enters the woods. The division darts team are expected to **lose** on Friday. There is a dangerous dog **loose** in the park.	It is surprising how often I see this mistake. People make mistakes with **loose** and **lose** because of the confusion over pronunciation. If you remember that **loose** rhymes with **moose**, you will eliminate this error.
I asked **myself** that question.	You cannot use *myself* for any other reason. You <u>cannot</u> use it because it sounds better than *me*. You <u>cannot</u> use it when someone other than "you" is doing something to

180

I said that **myself**.	"you." For example: *Pass any comments to the SIO or myself.* **X** It should be: *Pass any comments to the SIO or me.* Most often, writers make this mistake because they think 'myself' sounds more formal.
The victim **passed** his attacker without recognising him. The victim **walked past** his attacker without recognising him. The helicopter **passed** at an altitude of 100ft. The helicopter **flew past** at an altitude of 100ft.	If you have used a verb indicating motion already, then it will be partnered with *past* and not *passed*.
Have you taken **their** statements? The report is **there** on the desk.	The f**ir** is the**ir** f**ir** (mnemonic) **There** has another place word within it – t**here** **They're** means *there are*

They're bringing in the suspect now.	
I am going **to** court. I will come **too**. I'll meet you outside in **two** minutes.	Most people spell **two** correctly. The sound of the others should help you decide which to use– **too** is a longer sound than **to** so add another 'o'
. **Who** is in charge of this investigation. (Who is the subject of the verb to be.) No-one has seen the man **who** lives in this flat for three weeks. (*Who* is the subject of the verb *to live*.) You met with **whom** last night? She had a child **by whom**?	To check, substitute **who** with *he/she* or *they* and substitute **whom** with *him/her* or *them*. That part of the sentence should still make sense.
Where is the Connelly file? The new PCs **were** working together today.	Most people spell **wear** correctly. Where refers to place – you can see another word that refers to place within it –

You need to **wear** dress uniform for the ceremony.	w**here**. This might help you to remember which word to use.
We're going to arrest Billy Drake.	Contracted form of '**we are**'
Did you write **your** report? **You're** under arrest.	**You're** means *you are*; for anything else use **your**.
DI Miller **hung** his commendation on the wall. A man arrested for murdering his brother has been found **hanged** in his cell.	Curtains are **hung,** people are **hanged**

Exercise 4.12

Insert the correct words in the following sentences:

1. **affect or effect**

    - What will be the _____ of the latest cuts?
    - The whole family has been _____ed by the attack.

2. **its or it's**

    - _____ a pity you weren't here when the suspect was arrested.

183

- The sniffer dog returned to _____ master.

3.   **licence or license**

- I would like to see your _____ please.
- The premises are not _____ to sell alcohol.

4.   **loose or lose**

- We will _____ the case if the evidence is disallowed.
- The window frame was _____ so the burglar was able to enter.

5.   **past or passed**

- The thief ran _____ the police officer.
- The patrol car _____ the house every hour.

6. **practice or practise**

- I wonder if the new DCI will _____ what he preaches.
- Sgt Lomax looked forward to firing _____.

7. **there, their, they're**

- _____ both very good officers.
- DC Brown and DC Pemberton finished _____ reports on time.
- _____ is the house that was burgled.

8. **to, too, two**

- It's _____ hot in the interview room.
- The victims were _____ scared _____ report the muggings.

9. **were, where or we're**

- _____ _____ you at 6.30 yesterday evening?

185

- I wonder who the culprits _____.

- Tell the boss _____ on our way back to the station now.

10   your, you're

- You can give _____ statement here or at the station.
- _____ sure this is the man you saw?

Memory aids –

Mnemonics

We have seen how knowing a few rules and understanding how words are constructed can help with a whole variety of spelling queries. However, some people remember tricky spellings better with the aid of a rhyme or phrase called a mnemonic (the first 'm' is silent). Often it is better to work out one for yourself because they are easier to remember. This is particularly true in police writing, which has some complex and highly specialised words. There are some suggestions below that might get you started

ould – **o**h **u l**ucky **d**uck
- should

- could

- would

-

ound – **o**h **u n**aughty **d**uck
- ground

- found

- around

- sound

ie/ei

- I before E - except after C when the sound is 'ee'
- I before E- except after C, or when sounding like A as in neighbour or weigh, and except seize and seizure, weird, height, and either, their and neither.
- I before E, except after C -- don't we live in a weird society?

Even the mnemonics for this are confusing!

laugh – **l**augh **at** **u**gly **g**oat **h**air

because – **b**ig **e**lephants **c**an **a**lways **u**nderstand **s**mall **e**lephants

beautiful - **b**ig **e**lephants **a**re **u**sually **b**eautiful (for that tricky beginning)

island – an island **is** **land** surrounded by water

piece – a **pie**ce of **pie**
necessary – **1** **c**ollar and **2** **s**leeves are ne**c**e**ss**ary on a shirt

parliament – **liam** went to the houses of par**liam**ent

separate – never se**para**te a **para** from his **para**chute

secretary – a good **secret**ary can keep a **secret**

terrible – **rib**s taste ter**rib**le

business – going by **bus** is good **bus**iness

and my personal favourite:

diarrhoea – **d**oesn't **i**t **a**lways **r**un **r**ather **h**orribly **o**ver **e**ach **a**nkle

How to remember homophones

The best way to remember the difference in homophones is to make pictures in your head to help. For example:

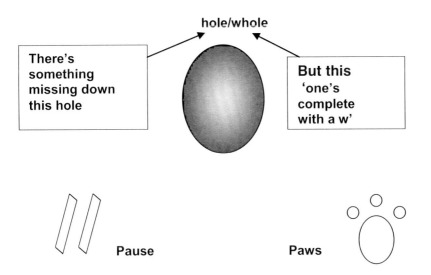

hole/whole

There's something missing down this hole

But this 'one's complete with a w'

Pause

Paws

Conclusion

In this chapter, we have seen the importance of correct spelling in police writing. Spelling is a very personal area to cover as each of us has our own spelling hurdles to get over. Having worked through this chapter, you will have hopefully discovered rules and tips to help you to remember the spellings of words that you find difficult.

I have included many of the problems that I have seen when marking written work submitted by police officers on my courses, but the criminal justice sector has some highly specialised words, often with Latin origins: *mens rea*, and *actus reus* for example. If you are concerned about these sector specific words (or any others for that matter) that you need to use in your daily writing tasks, you should buy a small indexed notebook and jot down any of the words that you find tricky. This would form your own personal dictionary of work related words. Having such a book to refer to will save you time when compiling your reports or statements. To get you started, I have included pages at the end of this book in which you can write some of your own workplace words for reference.

Answers

Exercise 4.1 - Spelling Self Assessment

Which of these options shows the correct spelling?

1) a. The accomodation in the cells is very basic?
   b. The accommodation in the cells is very basic? ✓
   c. The acommodation in the cells is very basic?

   (*you might remember **2 c**ots and **2 m**attresses*)

2) a. DC Mitchell's clothes for working undercover were bizaar.
   b. DC Mitchell's clothes for working undercover were bizzar.
   c. DC Mitchell's clothes for working undercover were bizarre. ✓

3) a. The shopkeeper definately saw Morton steal the phone.
   b. The shopkeeper definitly saw Morton steal the phone.
   c. The shopkeeper definitely saw Morton steal the phone. ✓

   (*it might help to split the word – de+finite+ly*)

4) a. It will be necessary for two officers to attend. ✓
   b. It will be neccessary for two officers to attend.
   c. It will be neccesary for two officers to attend.

*(reminder – it is **necessary** to have one c̲ollar and two s̲leeves on a shirt)*

5) a. PC Bryant will recieve a commendation for his bravery.
    b. PC Bryant will rieceve a commendation for his bravery.
    c. PC Bryant will receive a commendation for his bravery.
        ✓

6) a. The vehicle had been statianery for 30 minutes.
    b. The vehicle had been stationery for 30 minutes.
    c. The vehicle had been stationary for 30 minutes.   ✓

*(**station e̲ry** refers to paper goods– remember 'e' for envelopes)*

7) a. DI Mills will superceed the outgoing Det Supt.
    b. DI Mills will supercede the outgoing Det Supt.
 ✓ c. DI Mills will supersede the outgoing Det Supt.

*(Spelt with an **S**, because it comes from the Latin Super + Sedere)*

8) a. Do you think DC Wood will fullfil his early promise?
    b. Do you think DC Wood will fulfill his early promise?
    c. Do you think DC Wood will fulfil his early promise?   ✓

8) a. The patrol car is making a very wierd noise.
    b. The patrol car is making a very weard noise.
    c. The patrol car is making a very weird noise. ✓

(This is an exception to the rule "I before E, except after C")

9) a. The officers made the boys hand over they're knives.

b. The officers made the boys hand over their knives. ✓

c. The officers made the boys hand over there knives.

10) a. It is common practise for PCSOs to patrol the estate.

b. It is common practice for PCSOs to patrol the estate. ✓

c. It is common practis for PCSOs to patrol the estate.

(The words that end 'ce' are nouns and the words that end 'se' are verbs. Remember: **s**end (verb) for the **c**onstable (noun).

Exercise 4.2

ghoti – with reference to common phonological (sound) patterns in English, you could pronounce this in the same way as the word **fish.** Here is the logic:

'f' as in cou**gh**   'i' as in w**o**men   'sh' as in sta**ti**on

Exercise 3.3 - Read the following words and decide if the letter **y** has a vowel sound or a consonant sound. Write **v** or **c** in the box next to the word.

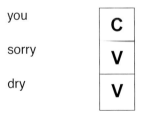

you

sorry

dry

beyond

silly

dynamite

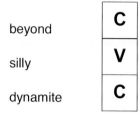

Exercise 4.4
Say each word aloud, count the number of syllables and write
it in e.g 3

London	2
Singapore	3
Manchester	3
Australia	4
France	1
Liverpool	3
Glasgow	2
Moscow	2
Spain	1
Argentina	4

Exercise 4.5 - Split the word in column 1 into prefix and base word.

Word	Prefix	Root
replace	re	place
misprint	mis	print
unusual	un	usual
immoral	im	moral
disagree	dis	agree
subway	sub	way
irregular	ir	regular
prefix	pre	fix

Exercise 4.6 - Split the word in column 1 into base word and suffix.

Word	Root	Suffix
quickly	quick	ly
thinking	think	ing
sweetest	sweet	est
wonderful	wonder	ful
hopeless	hope	less
darken	dark	en
cracked	crack	ed
employer	employ	er

Exercise 4.7

Check your knowledge of the main spelling terms: choose the best word to complete each sentence..

The word constable has three...

Select the word here	
	prefix
	suffix
	vowels
	consonants
✓	syllables
	long
	short

The underlined letters in constable are called...

Select the word here	
	prefix
	suffix
✓	vowels
	consonants
	syllables
	long
	short

The underlined letters in **c**o**nst**a**bl**e are called...

Select the word here	
	prefix
	suffix
	vowels
✓	consonants
	syllables
	long
	short

The vowel sound in **chase** is a ___ sound.

Select the word here	
	prefix
	suffix
	vowels
	consonants
	syllables
✓	long
	short

The vowel sound in **stab** is a ___ sound.

Select the word here	
	prefix
	suffix
	vowels
	consonants
	syllables
	long
✓	short

The underlined letters in enforce**ment** form the...

Select the word here	
	prefix
✓	suffix
	vowels
	consonants
	syllables
	long
	short

The underlined letters in **sub**poena form the...

Select the word here	
✓	prefix
	suffix
	vowels
	consonants
	syllables
	long
	short

Exercise 4.8

Join suffixes to these base words:

notice + able	noticeable
trouble + some	troublesome
enforce + ing	enforcing
certificate + ion	certification
impossible + ly	impossibly
expire + y	expiry
examine + ation	examination
expense + ive	expensive
size + able	sizeable
courage + ous	courageous

Exercise 4.9

Add the suffixes 'ed' and 'ing' to the following words commonly used in police reports:

Confer	conferred
	conferring
Occur	occurred
	occurring
Accelerate	accelerated
	accelerating
Testify	testified
	testifying
Caution	cautioned
	cautioning
Witness	witnessed
	witnessing
Argue	argued
	arguing
Bribe	bribed
	bribing
Admit	admitted
	admitting

** note that some of these words do not follow the rules discussed in this chapter. These are words that you might have to learn.

Add the suffix 'able' to the following words commonly used in police reports:

Regret	regrettable
Approach	approachable
Cite	citable
Arrest	arrestable
Enforce	enforceable

Add the suffix 'ment' to the following words commonly found in police reports:

Embezzle	embezzlement
Enforce	enforcement
State	statement
Assess	assessment
Judge	judgement/judgment

Exercise 4.10

Add the correct 'shun' endings to the base words in brackets below:

1. PC Golding told the man he had two _op**tions**_ , stop shouting or be arrested for disturbing the peace.

2. The evidence was found behind the new radiator in the _exten**sion**_.

3. His _rea**ction**_ to the news of his son's arrest was not as bad as I had expected.

4. Traffic was diverted because of a _colli**sion**_ on the motorway.

5. We had to call out an _electri**cian**_ to make the building safe before the officers could go in.

6. I get a great feeling of _satisfac**tion**_ when a crime is solved.

7. I had a _conversa**tion**_ with the DCI about increasing the size of the search team.

Exercise 4.11

Use a prefix to make the opposite of these words:

1. wrap **un**wrap

2.	use	**mis**use
3.	agree	**dis**agree
4.	engage	**dis**engage
5.	behave	**mis**behave
6.	understand	**mis**understand
7.	fold	**un**fold
8.	spell	**mis**spell
9.	connect	**dis**connect
10.	close	**dis**close

Exercise 4.12

Insert the correct words in the following sentences:

1. **affect or effect**

   - What will be the *effect* of the latest cuts?
   - The whole family has been *affected* by the attack.

2. **its or it's**

   - *It's* a pity you weren't here when the suspect was arrested.

- The sniffer dog returned to *its* master.

3.   **licence or license**

- I would like to see your *licence* please.
- The premises are not *licensed* to sell alcohol.

4.   **loose or lose**

- We will *lose* the case if the evidence is disallowed.
- The window frame was *loose* so the burglar was able to enter.

5.   **past or passed**

- The thief ran *past* the police officer.
- The patrol car *passed* the house every hour.

6.   **practice or practise**

- I wonder if the new DCI will *practise* what he preaches.
- Sgt Lomax looked forward to firing *practise*.

7.   **there, their, they're**

- *They're* both very good officers.
- DC Brown and DC Pemberton finished *their* reports on time.
- *There* is the house that was burgled.

8.   **to, too, two**

- It's *too* hot in the interview room.
- The victims were *too* scared *to* report the muggings.

9.   **were or where**

- *Where were* you at 6.30 yesterday evening?
- I wonder who the culprits *were*.
- Tell the boss *we're* on our way back to the station now.

10   **your, you're**

- You can give *your* statement here or at the station.
- *You're* sure this is the man you saw?

Chapter 5

The dos and don'ts of good report writing

Objectives

By the end of the chapter you will be able to:

- write in a clear professional style
- use the active and passive voice effectively
- write shorter, more concise sentences
- plan your writing

Introduction

In the first chapter we outlined the requirements of an effective police report. We saw that they should be: accurate, concise, objective, clear and complete. In subsequent chapters, we have seen how attention to grammar and punctuation can make writing clearer for the reader to understand and how accurate spelling helps to avoid misunderstandings. In this chapter we will consider police writing style.

Along with many other corporate writers, police officers adopt a style that is distinct. It contains a great deal of jargon; words are used in a unique way; sentences are long and complicated and the passive voice is used more often than necessary.

The answer to clear professional report writing is easy –

KISS
Keep it **s**imple and **s**traightforward

The following ten steps should help you to keep control of your writing, make it clear to your reader, keep it professional, and keep it concise whilst still complete. Remember, the role of your report is to communicate to all audiences clearly and without distractions.

1. Use the active voice

Although we considered this fully in Chapter 2 it is worth returning to it in this chapter. Many officers overuse the passive voice without really thinking about it, because they feel that it seems more formal. The truth is that not only is the active voice just as professional, it is clearer and active sentences contain fewer words.

Look at these examples in the passive voice:

- The matter will be investigated by us in due course.
- The riot was stopped by the police.
- The factory had to be closed by the senior fire officer.

These active sentences are much clearer because the people who did the action are at the beginning of the sentences:

- We will investigate the matter in due course.

- The police stopped the riot.
- The senior fire officer closed the factory.

As well as being clearer, you will also notice that the sentences are shorter. Each of the examples above is shorter by at least two words. This does not seem much, but that represents twenty words in ten such sentences. You can see how this would add up in a longer statement.

2.   Avoid 'policespeak'

Police officers at some point in the past have adopted a stilted style of writing with peculiar phraseology, almost a separate dialect. This seems to be passed on to newer officers during on the job training. Those of us who are not part of the criminal justice system (including most of the jury) find this style of writing very difficult to understand. Look at the following example:

"I alighted from my vehicle and asked the driver of the suspect vehicle, one Ms. Sofia Mills, to show her driving licence to myself."

You would probably not use this style of language when talking to a friend or maybe even a colleague, so why adopt this style in writing? Perhaps the officer here feels that using this particular terminology will make his/her writing more credible. However, this style of writing distracts the reader from what is being said. A clearer way of writing this would be:

208

"I got out of my patrol car and asked the driver, Ms. Sofia Mills, for her driving licence."

Everyone could understand this but it still maintains a level of formality and professionalism required for workplace writing.

Police writing is littered with complex phrases where a simple one would be more appropriate (deadwood words). Below are some suggestions for using clear simple language in place of some of the complicated terminology often preferred by police writers. I have picked out some of the common phrases I have come across during my work as a trainer. If you want more guidance The Plain English Campaign website has a booklet called the 'A-Z of Alternative Words'. You can download this and other writing guides free of charge from this address:

http://www.plainenglish.co.uk/free-guides.html.

Instead of…	Use…
advise	inform, tell, write
afford an opportunity	allow, permit, let
a great deal of the time	often
answer in the affirmative	say yes
aforesaid, aforementioned	this, these, earlier in this document
as a consequence of	because, as
are in receipt of	have received
as per	according to
at such time	when

at the present time	now
be advised	(avoid this term)
be in a position to	can
by means of	by, with
cognizance cognizant of	knowledge know
concur	agree
contingent upon the receipt of	When we receive
contacted	spoke to, visited, texted, phoned etc
direct effort towards	try
due to the fact that	because
during the course of during the time that	during while
excessive amount	too much
exit	leave, get out of
expedite	hasten, hurry, speed
for the purpose of	for, to
for the duration of	during, while
for the reason that	because
forthwith	now, at once
further to	following, after
give consideration to	consider, think about
have a need for	need
henceforth	from now on, in the future
hold in abeyance	wait
if and when	if or when (not both)
implement	carry out, set up
in a number of cases	some
in excess of	more than
in lieu of	instead of
in order that in order to	so to

in the affirmative	yes, agreed
in the very near future	soon
in the vicinity of	near
justification for	reason for
locality	place, area
(it is) mandatory	you must
make a decision	decide
make inquiry regarding	ask about
notwithstanding	despite, even if, still, yet
observed	saw
occasioned by	caused by
on the grounds that	because
on request	If you ask
optimum	the best, ideal
owing to the fact that	because
participate	take part
per diem, per annum	a day, a year
prior to	before
proceed	go
pursuant to	in line with, because of
reported	said
resided	lived
residence	house, flat, caravan
responded	answered
sibling	sister, brother
subsequently, subsequent to	after, later, then, next
sustained	received
take action	act
that being the case	if so
thereupon	then
transported	took, drove
ultimately	in the end, finally

until such time that	when
utilise	use
vehicle	car, van etc
with effect from	from
without further delay	immediately, soon (or say when)
with regard to with reference to with respect to	about, regarding, concerning
with the result that	so that

3.   Don't make the reader have to search for information

Many police officers make the reader have to look backwards or forwards in the narrative to gain information. For example, because the MG 11 usually has a section for a signature, date, and in some instances, time in the heading information, an officer will often begin their report by saying ' *on the above date and time, I was called to .....*'. This disrupts the flow of reading and makes it much harder for the reader to follow. It is better to repeat the information. An even worse practice it to refer to 'the below...' . This is really difficult for the reader because you are referring to information they have not yet seen. They must break off reading in order to find the information. The same applies to people's names; referring to the 'above named' or by allocating a number ie 'witness # 1' also means that your reader must search the document for the information. Remember the advice on writing narratives that we discussed in chapter 1. Your reader should be able to follow your narrative logically and clearly.

4.   Avoid overuse of nominalisation

When completing reports, some writers think that it sounds more formal and professional to use nominalisation. This is where you convert a **verb** into a **noun** and then add a **verb** to take the place of the one that you converted. Confused? Look at these examples:

- The officers **took action** to contain the situation.
- We had a **discussion** about the new rotas.
- The **implementation** of the Policing Protocol was done by a designated team.

It is much clearer and just as professional to use the first verb:

- The officers acted to contain the situation.
- We discussed the new rotas.
- A designated team implemented the Policing Protocol.

Of course, this does not mean that you should never use nominaliation; they can add objectivity to some sentences. My advice is not to overuse them in your writing. A quick check is to look out for 'ion' endings and consider if you need all of them.

5.   Steer clear of the never-ending sentence/paragraph

Once again, in an attempt to sound more formal, some police officers tend to use long sentences containing several dependant clauses in the form of qualifying phrases. Look at this example:

- The victim, an eighteen year old female, said, although she was not quite sure of other facts because it had happened so quickly, that her assailant, who had attacked her from behind, was a tall, strong male wearing red and blue gloves, which she could see clearly, although briefly, when he tried to put his hand over her mouth.

This sentence is 59 words long. It is very difficult to extract the information from it. It would be clearer if the information were given in separate sentences:

- The victim is an eighteen-year-old female. She said that her assailant was a tall strong man who was wearing red and blue gloves. She could see these clearly when he tried to put his hands over her mouth.

Long complicated sentences are not an effective way to communicate especially in the case of statements that are read out in court. There is a tendency in such sentences to lose track of what needs to be incorporated, resulting in unnecessary information being included.

Similarly, overlong paragraphs are less successful than shorter carefully thought out ones. Many people are unsure about paragraph demarcation but you can see from your work in Chapter 2, Section E, that clear paragraphs guide your reader through your report and give them time to digest each of your points in a logical way.

6.   **Beware acronyms, abbreviations and slang**

When talking to or emailing colleagues, or others familiar with the language of policing, you will probably use quite a number of acronyms: RTA, C&C, CPS, IPI for example. In fact, there are so many acronyms in policing that many officers have said that they get confused sometimes. This is because these can differ from force to force or the same acronym can have more than one meaning; the acronym SC can stand for Security Check, Special Constable or Specialist Crime.

Similarly, abbreviations such as 'obbo' (observation) and 'mis per' (missing persons) and slang such as snitch (informer) and jumper (a thief who steals from offices) may be unfathomable from one department to another and will almost certainly be incomprehensible to the average layperson.

Remember, people who are not familiar with police language will read your writing. Such jargon will make them feel alienated, and they are likely to view your report less positively. If you must use an abbreviation because it will be repeated several times, write the term in full the first time and place the acronym in brackets, for example Police Support Unit (PSU); you can then just use the acronym in the rest of the report.

Swearing is a part of everyday language for many people today and has become commonplace. Many situations that police officers find themselves in are stressful and emotionally charged but profanity at any level should not be included unless it is reported speech. However, some words are used so commonly, they have lost their impact. These words then find their way into police reports. Incidents of this are usually spotted during checking, but not always. Look, for example, at the extract below from a police statement that is now in the public domain:

'I bollocked him and he was dragged away'

The use of this slang term makes the writer appear unprofessional. There are a number of alternative terms that could have been used here: remonstrated, berated, reproached.

7.   **Write what you mean**

Most of us, in casual conversation use informal colloquial phrases that convey a meaning beyond the actual words that are said, for example 'can't see the wood for the trees', 'taking the mickey' and 'come a cropper'. In our everyday language, some of these phrases reflect our dialect and culture and add colour to our language, whilst others become overused or meaningless buzz words such as 'over the moon', 'blue sky thinking' and 'strategic staircase'.

In addition, we might use euphemisms as a polite or diplomatic way of saying something especially when investigating or reporting on sex crimes or when dealing with sensitive topics, for example, private parts instead of penis; weight problem instead of obese; uncooperative instead of refused to answer.

However you view idioms, such imprecise phrases have no place in police reports; the words you write should mean exactly what they say. Avoiding this informal language will ensure that your meaning is obvious, even to those who have not learnt these common idioms. These might include those for whom English is a second language. No matter how proficient people are in a second language, some of these idioms (particular local ones) can prove to be a barrier to clear understanding. In addition, some police reports might be read many years later, such as those from Hillsborough. Some of these phrases might have changed meaning or gone out of use.

Always remember that your writing is a permanent and public record of an event and your actions within it. Your meaning must not depend upon the whims of fashion and your local dialect. It should mean precisely what you have written.

8   Before and after – planning and proofreading

Many police officers that I have spoken to say that they just don't have time to do a plan before they write, but trust me, it actually saves time in the long run. If you 'think' on screen or as you write, even with the help of your notes, you might remember things that should have been included earlier in your account. This means going back and inserting additional material or cutting and pasting information. This process can disrupt the grammar or the cohesion of your writing, making it very difficult to understand clearly. In addition, information can be left out or end up out of order. All of this could result in reports being returned for rewriting, or worse, challenged in court.

Planning does not have to be a lengthy process. A simple bulleted list would help you to remember all of your points. You could number these in order of importance once your list is completed. Alternatively a simple flow chart would help you to plot a sequence of events. My personal favourite is to write points/events on sticky notes; I can then rearrange them into the order that I want them to appear in my writing (I worked through many packs during the writing of this book).

Similarly, proofreading is a vital part of the writing process. Although computer spelling and grammar checkers are a useful starting point, they don't pick up every error. Many people, including myself, find it difficult to proofread their own work, especially when time is tight and a report needs to be handed in quickly. This is because you know what you meant to write so as you read it through, your brain fills in many of the gaps. The ideal situation would be to ask someone else to check it for you. If this is not possible, try reading it backwards, sentence by sentence. This 'tricks' your brain into thinking that you are reading it for the first time; you are more likely to spot errors this way.

An officer in one of my classes said that he never bothered to proofread his work because he felt it was his supervisor's responsibility to check and return it if there were errors. Although I can see the logic in this argument, my answer would be that it is not his supervisor that would be made a fool of in court if mistakes had been missed.

9 American or English?

We have looked closely at spelling in chapter four, but there is much heated debate about the use of American spellings such as 'organization' rather than 'organisation', with some people feeling quite strongly about the subject. If it makes any of you feel any better, the 'ize' spelling was the original English spelling from the Greek root. We later changed it to the French 'ise' spelling, not the other way round. Any of you that have an Oxford English dictionary will notice that they list the 'ize' version.

Today either form is acceptable in formal business writing as long as it is consistent throughout your report. Having said that, some departments do set a 'house style' with a preference for one form, so you should check with a supervisor if you move departments.

10 Use the three-step method in your note taking.

On many occasions, your report starts with the notes that you take at the time of the event. If you adopt the following three-step approach whenever possible, you will save time and increase the quality of your report.

1. Listen to the witness's account without writing anything down. This allows you to

   a. keep the witness on track with the narrative
   b. find out exactly what has happened

c. listen for any untruthfulness or discrepancies
d. decide what action to take

2. Ask the witness to retell the account and you take notes. This allows you to

a. gather information about the incident
b. ask questions as you guide the witness through the story
c. establish the chronological order of events
d. establish the facts

If you think about the structure of the report that you will have to write, you can ask your guiding questions in the same order. This will organise your report as you take your notes, saving time and avoiding information being missed out later.

3. Read your notes to the witness

When you read your notes in this way, you are reading what you will later write in your report. This allows you to

a. correct any errors
b. add further information the witness might have remembered
c. ask any final questions

Using this method whenever appropriate can add credibility to your report as evidence. If there is a discrepancy between your report and the witness evidence in court, a structured method such as this documents your actions during that vital stage.

Conclusion

These ten tips act as a quick reference point for improving your writing and for advising others. Integrating some of these steps in your workplace writing should improve quality and clarity, resulting in writing that is professional, complete and accessible to the wide range of audiences who must understand it.

Last word from the author

I hope that you have found this book helpful and that all of your concerns have been addressed. If you still have any questions on any of the topic areas covered, or if you have any suggestions for addition in future editions, please contact me on info@ellis-hall.co.uk, I will do my best to help.

If you would like further practice on some of the skills included in the book, you might find the following websites useful:

http://www.bbc.co.uk/skillswise/english

This site has explanations, exercises and games to help you with the underpinning skills related to spelling, punctuation and grammar. The link is for the English section but there is also a maths area that can be accessed from it. Although it was developed for adults, this might also be a useful site for those of you who might have to support children with homework.

http://www.skillsworkshop.org/literacy

This site is aimed at adults across a range of levels, you should choose L1 if you wanted a reminder of a topic and L2 to progress

https://www.tes.co.uk/secondary-teaching-resources

This site is aimed at secondary school students but there are some good practice materials plus Powerpoint presentations for further explanation. I have given the link to all the secondary resources in case you wanted to explore other subjects for supporting children. You can also access primary resources here. The site, like the others, is free but you need to register. You will be prompted to do this when you try to open a resource.

The book has been proofread by a number of people, myself included. However, despite how thoroughly this process is carried out, some mistakes can be overlooked. If you do spot any, please accept my apologies. I would be grateful if you would contact me on the address above to point them out so that they can be corrected.

Finally, I would love to hear what you think about the book. If you enjoyed it and found it useful, it is always good to hear. If you have any criticisms, I would like to hear those too. If the problem is something that I can fix, I will do so. You can contact me at ann.ellis@ellis-hall.co.uk

It only remains for me to wish you good luck in your future career.

References

- *High level Ploddledygook tops jargon charts with 102-word sentence, 2009:*

  http://www.plainenglish.co.uk/news/974-high-level-ploddledygook-tops-jargon-charts-with-102-word-sentence.html Last viewed 3/8/2015

- More training required on stop and search,

  http://www.policemag.co.uk/editions/april15_news_more_training.aspx (author not given) last viewed 3/8/2015

- Patrick C Notchtree (date unknown). One Easy Rule: http://www.dreaded-apostrophe.com/ Last viewed 3/8/2015

- Truss, L (2009). Eats, shoots and leaves: London, Harper and Collins

- Witness Statement, http://present.brighton-hove.gov.uk/Published/C00000160/M00002197/AI00007608/Item129apdxg.pdf (date and author unknown) last viewed 3/8/2015

- Zar, JH (1992). Candidate for a Pullet Prize: *The Journal of Irreproducible Results*, Vol. 45, No. 5/6, 2000, page 20. See www.jir.com/pullet.html.

Personal Dictionary of workplace words

These pages have been added for you to write down any workplace words that you find troublesome. Keep it for your own reference.

Word	meaning
----------------------------------	----------------------------------
----------------------------------	----------------------------------
----------------------------------	----------------------------------
----------------------------------	----------------------------------
----------------------------------	----------------------------------
----------------------------------	----------------------------------
----------------------------------	----------------------------------
----------------------------------	----------------------------------
----------------------------------	----------------------------------
----------------------------------	----------------------------------
----------------------------------	----------------------------------
----------------------------------	----------------------------------
----------------------------------	----------------------------------
----------------------------------	----------------------------------
----------------------------------	----------------------------------
----------------------------------	----------------------------------

Word	meaning
--------------------------------	--------------------------------
--------------------------------	--------------------------------
--------------------------------	--------------------------------
--------------------------------	--------------------------------
--------------------------------	--------------------------------
--------------------------------	--------------------------------
--------------------------------	--------------------------------
--------------------------------	--------------------------------
--------------------------------	--------------------------------
--------------------------------	--------------------------------
--------------------------------	--------------------------------
--------------------------------	--------------------------------
--------------------------------	--------------------------------
--------------------------------	--------------------------------
--------------------------------	--------------------------------
--------------------------------	--------------------------------

Word	meaning
------------------------------	------------------------------
------------------------------	------------------------------
------------------------------	------------------------------
------------------------------	------------------------------
------------------------------	------------------------------
------------------------------	------------------------------
------------------------------	------------------------------
------------------------------	------------------------------
------------------------------	------------------------------
------------------------------	------------------------------
------------------------------	------------------------------
------------------------------	------------------------------
------------------------------	------------------------------
------------------------------	------------------------------
------------------------------	------------------------------
------------------------------	------------------------------
------------------------------	------------------------------

Index